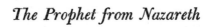

The Prophet from Nazareth

Books by Morton Scott Enslin

The Ethics of Paul
Christian Beginnings
The Prophet from Nazareth

THE PROPHET
FROM NAZARETH

BY MORTON SCOTT ENSLIN

McGRAW-HILL BOOK COMPANY, INC. New York Toronto London

R. T. E.

T. V. E.   M. S. E.

P. E. M.   J. R. M.

Felices ter et amplius
Quos irrupta tenet copula, nec, malis
Divulsus quærimoniis,
Suprema citius solvet amor die.

Contents

Εἰ γάρ τι καλὸν ἔργον πεποίηκα,
τοῦτο μνημεῖόν ἐστιν· εἰ δὲ μηδέν,
οὐδ᾽ οἱ πάντες ἀνδριάντες.

Prolegomena: *"In the fifteenth year of Tiberius"*

THIS BOOK is in no sense a Life of Jesus. To write such is impossible. Through the years many such attempts have been made. They have all been failures. We simply do not have the materials. The four gospels, which now stand securely at the beginning of the New Testament, are among the most important books ever penned because of their influence in moulding the thought and shaping the culture of a very sizable part of the world. They are, nonetheless, not biographies of Jesus or sources from which a biography can be drawn. The earliest of them was not written until at least a full generation after his tragic death. When they were written, their function was to make saints, not historians. There was little thought and less concern for preserving facts for coming ages which might wish to be informed. There would be no coming age for which to write. At any moment the long-deferred promise of God, treasured through the years and at long last finally announced afresh by God's specially designated herald, their Lord, would be realized.

1

The present age would vanish, and a new world would appear in which the herald would return to be seen and recognized by all men as Lord and King.

When the gospels were written, apparently during the last thirty years of the first century, the authors, no one of whom was himself an eyewitness of the events he was seeking to record, were dependent upon materials which had accumulated through the years of mission preaching, as zealous followers of the crucified prophet sought to continue his work of proclaiming the momentary coming of the expected kingdom. Among these materials were undoubtedly reminiscences of things which he had said and done, preserved, however, not for future biographers but because they were useful to missionary preachers, buttressing their warnings and giving urgency to their appeals. Apparently first in the form of detached "And he said's" and "And he did's," this growing mass of tradition was essentially what may be styled "sermon helps" or illustrative material used to add light and give authority to the preachers' spoken words.

Then, as now, such materials were not preserved unchanged. To fit and point a particular insistence an illustrative story may well need some adaptation. Thus the material changed, some incidents and emphases dropping out of sight, others being developed or added *de novo*.

Not only form but content changed. While Jesus was with his disciples he may well have been a complete answer to their questions. They were sure they knew who he was. It was impossible to fail to understand what he meant. His tragic death changed that circumstance, and dramatically. With his removal from them and due to their unshakable confidence in him as one sent and blessed by God, a new question arose which seemed to demand an answer: "Who, then, was he?" and answers continued to be given, not only in the early months but through the succeeding years. We call the results "Christology," a term which sums up the many attempted identifications of the one who now so completely gripped their lives and whose grip upon them his death had but tightened.

By the time our gospels appeared, this inevitable attempt to answer the questions which his impress upon them had made so insistent was well under way, and in the gospels some of the answers—the identifications—are plain to see: Son of man, Son of God, Messiah, Lord, the Suffering Servant glimpsed by the Prophet of the Exile, the pre-existent creative Word, through whom "all that hath been made was made." In short, the religion *of* Jesus was speedily transformed into the religion *about* Jesus. With this change Jesus was more and more coming to be seen as the embodiment and guarantee of men's most persistent longings and dreams.

When the evangelists produced their books, they were, again greatly to simplify, far more theologians than they were historians, for they were concerned with interpreting and explaining the divine significance and meaning of the incidents—the man and his message—which they were now braiding together, not with simply recording them. To change the figure, they were artists, not photographers, and into their portraits they painted, as all true artists do, far more than their physical eyes had seen.

It is accordingly not strange that our gospels show unmistakable evidence of this search for values, the result of the attempt to explain and appraise this figure whom men were so sure had been sent by God. It is this which leads the historian who allows his findings to determine his feelings to regard our gospels as far more reliable in reflecting the thinking of the age which saw their birth than in preserving a severely factual and unaltered précis of the sayings and doings of the one who had preached by Galilee's lake and in Jerusalem's streets.

Thus it is manifestly impossible to write a "life of Jesus." It has been said, and rightly: "We do not have enough material to write a respectable obituary notice." Yes, if by that we mean precisely dated and completely unreworked "material." Even the basic outline of his life, as it now stands in our first three gospels—largely the product of that too long minimized and devoted artist, the author of the gospel we style "according to Mark"—is far from chronologically accurate in the sense of a precise sequence of actual events. Here for the first time is the attempt to join together in a connected sequence the many "And he said's" and "And he did's," few, if any, of which carried with them any indication of the where and the when and the why. Nor is there any likelihood that Mark was concerned to find answers to these interrogatives, which in later years were to pique the reader's curiosity. The ability and consummate craftsmanship of this first compiler were devoted to attempting the answer to what was to him the burning question: "Why, if Jesus was what he was, did men do to him what they did?" Mark's answer is crystal-clear: "Because they did not know." The reason for the treatment which Jesus had received was ignorance: no one knew who he was. Only the twelve disciples had gained any insight, and theirs was but partial. Clear sight, even for them, came only in the light of the Resurrection. The rest of the people could not see at all. It was because of this ignorance that the rulers had put him to death; the rank and file of the populace were not concerned enough even to protest.

Thus the earliest attempt at a connected story is dominated by a theological, not a historical, concern. The later gospels, Matthew and Luke, provide the historian who would like to sketch the actual life of Jesus no help, for they take over bodily Mark's quite artificial and theologically determined outline of events; and into this outline they insert their extra material, largely in the form of parables and sayings which tradition had brought down to them, many in a far from unaltered form, but instead revealing the pondering and questioning of the years.

Here, then, is the reason for our inability to reconstruct the life of Jesus: we have no sources from which to draw. To many these results of careful and devoted study of the gospels and of their central figure have been both painful and disillusioning. "The critics have taken away our Jesus" has been the repeated protest, which echoes the word of Mary Magdalene on the first Easter morning: "They have taken away my Lord, and I know not where they have laid him." [1]

To others the results of a century and a half of critical study, with its inescapable conclusion that it is impossible to reconstruct the life of Jesus, has brought a different and more alarming attitude. They "accept the findings of critical scholarship" a bit too easily, as if that verdict were "it is impossible to know anything about Jesus," which is far more than the findings of critical scholarship do assert. Worse than that, they accept the conclusion almost jauntily: "It doesn't matter much anyhow." In place of the historical Jesus, whom they assume it is impossible to discover, and thus for whom further search is an unwarranted waste of time, they set the figure of the Eternal Christ and his part in the all-central epic of salvation—the technical term is *Heilsgeschichte*—which comprise the one and only important chapter of all cosmic history.

One searches in vain in the writings of many of the cham-

[1] John 20:13.

pions of what is commonly styled neoörthodoxy for any attempt to discover the Jesus of history. In the most literal sense he seems dispensable. The prologue to the Gospel of John, the cross on Calvary and its subsequent supernatural reversal—yes, these are featured. But even these events are seemingly removed afar from the realm of history. No heed is paid to what led up to the crucifixion, to the events which must be styled the political and ecclesiastical causes of the tragedy on the hill. Instead this all-decisive moment is simply a part of a heavenly scenario, contrived and stage-managed by God alone. Pilate, outraged chief priests, Herod, Peter— none of them is an actual flesh-and-blood character. Rather they seem actually stage properties. For the rest of the story there is seemingly neither interest nor concern.

To both of these attempts—the indignant outcry of protest and the seemingly unconcerned readiness to substitute a "just as good"—the same answer must be given: You have failed to read the evidence with understanding. It is indeed impossible to reconstruct a life or biography of Jesus of Nazareth; but it is entirely possible to gain a very clear picture of the sort of man he was, of his fundamental concern for and his complete dedication to what he passionately believed God's will for him and his fellows to be, and of the tremendous influence he exerted. Not only is it possible; it is well worth the doing. The critics have not taken away the actual Jesus of history. What they have done is to show the unreality of the Jesus who has been superficially read out of the gospels, transformed into the glorified image and likeness of each generation which has attempted so to do, and then read back again into the gospel pages. That Jesus has vanished. The critics have not destroyed him. They have simply shown that he never existed.

The quest for the real Jesus, the one who laid his hand of

compulsion upon those with whom he came in contact, and who so influenced those who knew him that they sought to carry on where he left off—this quest is possible. If the quest is to be successful, it must start on the right path. The one all-important fact to be kept before the eye is that the story which climaxed on Calvary was no theatre piece played on the stage of a heavenly Armageddon, but a very real and human conflict which occurred on the soil of a frontier province of the Roman empire, where life, though very different, was just as real and perplexing as is what we are experiencing today. We read such phrases as "in the days of Herod the king," "in the fifteenth year of Tiberius," and ". . . they carried him away, and delivered him up to Pilate"; but too often they are just "Bible names," like Melchizedek and Gabriel. So often we have added to the word, "he was in the world," the seemingly pious and proper theological conclusion, "but he was not of the world," that we have actually come to believe it. So we have looked for some one who was not there and missed the one who was.

It comes as a shock to many to be told that Jesus had far more in common with the Jews of his own day and land than he would with most Christians today who so lavishly praise him; that he talked about matters which his fellows knew and understood. The words, "kingdom of God," "repentance," "end of the age," "age to come," "resurrection," are common in the gospel pages. Never do we find Jesus asked by his hearers, friendly or critical, what these terms mean or forced to explain them.

We may find some of them obscure; his hearers did not. The anger of the ones, the devotion of the others, were not due to not knowing what he meant, but to knowing—in some cases all too well. In a very literal, if limited, sense of the word, "his ways were their ways and his thoughts their thoughts." When he spoke of Moses as author of the Pentateuch, or David of the Psalms, he meant it. When he spoke of people tormented by the residence within them of evil spirits, he was not disguising a knowledge of modern subliminal consciousness or of depth psychology. He really thought the demons there. In the mistaken, if natural, attempt to make "our Lord know at least as much as we do," we have tended to deprive him not only of his flaming concern for his fellow Jews, to whom he believed he had been sent by God to speak words which they must hear, but also of essential moral integrity, by portraying him as purporting to believe what he knew to be false.

In approaching any figure of the past, the first lesson the seeker must learn, if he is to have any hope for success in his quest, is what to look for. It seems so fair and dispassionate to say: "He shall answer my questions exactly as he wills; I will in no wise try to weight or slant his answers." But such an approach is doomed to failure. If we would understand the past and its figures, we must not obtrude our questions. Rather, it is our task to see what questions they were raising and how they answered them. One of the reasons the Jesus of history has eluded us, when he did not elude or seem obscure to those with whom he lived and worked, is that we have tried to make him at home in our world and concerned with our particular problems. He did not live in twentieth-century America, but in first-century Palestine. He was talking to the men and women of that day about his concerns and theirs. He was not talking to us over their heads, pretending an interest in them but really concerned with us.

It may have been natural for a past generation to ponder and debate the question, "What would Jesus do?" as they sought to solve their problems. Such attempts could not—

and did not—fail to make him unreal. It sometimes comes as a shock, but a wholesome one, that had what we call the "incarnation" taken place in New York or Boston in the year of grace 1960, instead of in Roman Palestine during the first three decades of the Christian era, Jesus would neither have worn a tunic and sandals nor spoken Aramaic. Equally certain it is that he would have talked about many quite different matters and had many different opinions on many subjects, very probably not excepting some about which he then did speak.

Thus our failure to see the man whom we have been looking for and the decision that he was, to cite a flashy best seller which appeared a generation ago, *The Man Nobody Knows*, are in no small part due to the fact that we have not been looking in the right direction, have not known what to look for. We have used the four gospels as if they were a series of unedited and unretouched pictures. They are not. Instead they are cabinets of artists' portraits, and bear clear evidence of that fact. We cannot reconstruct from them a biography of the man; but, when they are rightly studied, we can see the man himself, one who made so deep and lasting an impression as to make inevitable a series of answers and explanations of the central question: Who, then, was he? Many of these interpretations are closer to poetry than to unedited prose. They do not contribute material for a biography; yet in a real sense they are a part of his life. It was due to the impress he made on those who knew him that the subsequent materials came to be associated with him and to seem so natural and proper. There is such a thing as the immortality of influence.

In the quest for the real Jesus the student will soon become convinced that if he is to see the man himself, much in the gospel record must be laid to one side as later accretion. But he should be aware of its nature and its worth. It is here that so many well-meaning but nonetheless incompetent critics of the critics take needless alarm. The permanent values of the layers of accumulation, if values they are, are not destroyed or lessened when so appraised. To view them as valueless *fragments*, though frequently done, is shortsighted, even stupid. One example must suffice.

It will be generally conceded without argument that the three chapters in Matthew [2] which are commonly styled the "Sermon on the Mount" stand very high on the list of truly significant insights and pronouncements. Without them we should be far poorer. Now in the mature and reverent judgment of many—not to say most—students of the gospels, whose opinions are the result of long and detailed study, it is certain that this "Sermon" is not a unit in the sense that it was delivered by Jesus at a given time. Instead, it is highly composite, a mosaic of many sayings produced at different times and under very different circumstances. Some of the words may well reflect in varying degree words actually spoken by Jesus to hearers in Palestine. Others with equal certainty must be assigned to subsequent voices. In a word, the Sermon as we have it may well be one of the homiletic masterpieces of all time. It is nonetheless an example of the homiletic skill of "Matthew," not of Jesus. It is unnecessary to argue this conclusion point by point. The demonstration has already been made and can be read by those who will take the trouble so to do.[3] The point of importance is that this conclusion, which the nature of the evidence demands, does not in the slightest degree despoil

[2] Matt. 5–7.
[3] Cf. Martin Dibelius, *The Sermon on the Mount;* Hans Windisch, *The Meaning of the Sermon on the Mount;* Amos N. Wilder, "The Sermon on the Mount" in *The Interpreter's Bible,* Vol. 7, pp. 155–164.

the beauty or limit the value of the Sermon. It is still in the New Testament and in the conscience of most people who know it as an imperishable challenge and an abiding store of treasure.

What is true of the Sermon on the Mount is true of the host of other items in the gospels. The unthinking protest that the critic has torn the Bible to pieces and has thrown most of its contents away is without foundation. All of the contents remain, and the values remain values for those to whom the word, "God has still more light to break forth," has meaning.

Accordingly, the quest of the real Jesus need not be abandoned in consequence of a fear that it is hopeless—we can never see him—or that it is too dangerous and costly— it can only end in destroying values. Of course, the man who starts on the quest with the honest determination to follow the evidence wherever it leads and to accept the conclusions which the seeming facts demand will speedily discover that much, perhaps most, of what has come to be regarded as part of the central historical figure is not, strictly speaking, such, but has grown and become attached and entwined through the years. He will not have gone very far before he discovers that this process of accumulation started in the earliest days; that long before the gospels were produced it had been going on.

He will also discover two other matters of great import: that the part of the growth which is of permanent value remains of value quite regardless of its immediate origin; and that it is folly to wish to discard it as something later and therefore spurious, even as it is folly to try to separate the waters of the Mississippi near its delta and to reject all as "spurious and worthless" which did not start out of Little

Elk Lake in northern Minnesota. From its start Christianity
has been a stream, constantly fed by tributaries, not a pool
without intake or outlet.

The other discovery he will likely make at some stage in
the quest is of equal moment. It is this. Though he will never
succeed in his search, will never find the "historical Jesus"
in such a way as to satisfy folk accustomed to conventional
biographies, he will catch glimpses, if his eye be keen and he
wide-awake, which will convince him of the greatness of
the one of whom he is in quest, and of the impact he made
upon his world.

He may become increasingly uncertain as to exact details,
may even hesitate to single out any particular saying or
incident of which he will be ready to say, "This is an original,
unretouched bit," for by that time the searcher will probably
have become convinced that from the very first the portrayers
of Jesus were artists, not photographers. Nonetheless he will
probably be confident that in the materials there is much
which is in the truest sense "original," even though he may
be unable with precision to isolate or reproduce it. At times
he may even think a bit whimsically of the old story of the
captain and his silver teapot. Had he lost the teapot? Indeed no! He knew just where it was. It was at the bottom of
the ocean.

He will be unwilling to say of this saying or that, regardless of how primitive it sounds, that it must be put within
quotation marks as an exact word preserved unchanged, for
he will realize that during the years between the ministry
and the writing of the gospels the material had been preserved, not to pass on to posterity—there would be no
"posterity"; the Lord would return at any moment—but as
words to use in mission preaching to the unconverted. Many

an "And he said this . . ." or "And he did that . . ." must have
been inevitably, if unconsciously, altered as it was translated
not only from Aramaic to Greek, but from the thinking of
little Palestine to that of the far wider outside world into
which the preachers went.

But he will be certain—at least he will if his quest has
been at all like mine—that the figure who so eludes his later
grasp did not elude those among whom he moved. They
may have failed to evaluate him aright, may have been
baffled, repulsed, relentlessly hostile; but that their varying
estimates stemmed from ignorance of what Jesus was talking about, he will not accept. It was because they knew, not
because they did not, that they acted as they did.

He will likely become convinced—it is hard to see how
he can escape that discovery too, if he reads with his mind
as well as his eyes—that at times in the history of the world
there have become accumulated huge heaps of flammable
materials. He will discover such a heap near the beginning
of the first Christian century: Jewish Messianism, the age-
old promise of God of the golden age sure to come and in
vivid contrast to the sorry plight of the chosen people in
endless slavery; failure of nerve in the Mediterranean world,
due to the collapse of earlier dreams and confidence; increasing unrest and passionate longing for security and assurance.
Yes, a huge pile was ready to hand. But he will realize that
such piles rarely take flame of themselves; and he will likely
ask, "Who scratched the match?"

From then on the path will become more plain, for one
thing will stand out in increasing clearness: the direct impact, the influence, upon his fellows of this man who seems
to have started the conflagration. He may well wish that
he knew a better word than the prosy and too-overworked

term "personality," for he will become increasingly certain that here lies the real end and goal of his quest, a quest well worth the labor, sweat, and tears which it may have cost.

Against this background of misunderstanding and uncertainty, and in the confidence that there are many today who will wish to join those long devoted to this quest, this book is written. Its thesis is: (1) All who heard Jesus understood him. His enemies sent him to the cross, not because they did not know what he meant, but because they did. His first followers braved the same opposition which had cost him his life and sounded his word at home and abroad because they knew what he had meant and had accepted it as the very word of God. (2) While we cannot write a biography, we can know the man, can see him engaged in a life-and-death struggle, in the midst of real men, enemies and friends alike, not lifeless puppets seeming to move on the silver screen of an altogether-other Cinerama *in vacuo theologico.* (3) Far from being dispensable, a figure cavalierly to be dismissed as inconsequential then, irrelevant now, he stands ever demanding from his followers the same commitment and devotion to their tasks which he brought to his.

1

"We have no king but Caesar"

As the climax to a story which for dramatic power has never been surpassed we see a lonely wind-swept hill. In the bleak darkness loom three crosses. From the one in the centre comes a terrible cry—and then in an instant all is still.

That scene has never been forgotten, and never will. Within a score of years the Cross on the Hill had become for an ever-increasing group of people the turning point in history. And the cry from the darkness becomes strangely changed. Instead of the word, "My God, my God, why hast thou forsaken me?"[1] from the one who had been confident to the last that as God's chosen prophet he had but sounded the Father's will, and who had received his pay for it in a bitter cup, there came to stand the far more congenial words, first: "Father, into thy hands I commend my spirit"[2]; then: "It is finished."[3]

To many this change in wording has seemed most fitting.

[1] Mark 15:34; Matt. 27:46.   [2] Luke 23:46.   [3] John 19:30.

15

To others it is a mistaken anticlimax. Though the word, also put upon his lips by those who sought to do him honor, "I have overcome the world," [4] speedily came to a literal fulfillment (as the saying, "Vicisti, Galilæe," [5] attributed to the dying emperor Julian, attests), those who regret the altered word know that it is *not* "finished" and never will be; that instead the road still stretches on to the far horizon.

One thing is very clear. In all our reflections upon the significance of the Cross on the Hill we should never forget, as theology seemingly is wont to do, that had it not been for the days around the Galilean lake and in Jerusalem's streets, there would never have been the cross on Calvary's hill. It was the confidence in him—the confidence that he was "a man sent from God"—felt by those who knew him, that led to the one all-important conviction, without which there would never have been a memory in succeeding generations and ages of a Cross on the Hill. And this conviction, held by the followers of the crucified prophet, despite their cowardly flight at the time of crisis, was that it was unthinkable that he had been in error in his claim to be God's mouthpiece as he had proclaimed the good news of the impending fulfillment of the long and strangely deferred promise of God. Thus, of necessity, God had blessed—not cursed, as Golgotha seemed at first to suggest—both the man and his mission. No quest for the Jesus of history—whose impress

---

[4] John 16:33.

[5] This so-to-speak deathbed confession is utterly improbable; but what he is made to deplore was sober and incontrovertible truth. The earliest form of the story is given by the fifth-century Theodoret (*Hist. Eccl.* iii, 25, 7). Montaigne (*Essais* ii, 19— "Of Liberty of Conscience") discussed it in some detail and concluded sensibly that the silence of Ammianus Marcellinus and Eutropius renders its historicity most unlikely. The poet Swinburne adapted the word to the well-known "Thou hast conquered, O pale Galilean; the world has grown gray from thy breath" (*Hymn to Proserpine*).

upon his hearers made natural, even inevitable, his subsequent transformation into their Christ of faith—can hope for success if it starts from the cross. What led to the later confidence in the saving power of his death was the devotion which had been aroused by the nature and impress of his life. I confess it has long seemed to me proper that when a later Christian [6] sought to memorialize the real turning point in human history, which he was convinced had been divinely planned, he did not seek the date of the death, but of the birth of Jesus, as the proper point of start.

That ever during his lifetime Jesus was as much as a hundred miles from home is most improbable. Born in a little village unnoticed by ancient writers, some fifty miles north of Jerusalem, he lived and died in a little land scarcely larger than the state of Massachusetts, crowded in between the eastern end of the Mediterranean and the Syrian desert. The checkered history of this land was largely colored, if not actually determined, by its location at the western end of what has long been aptly styled "the fertile crescent"—a narrow strip of arable and easily traveled land forming a natural bridge and highway between two great areas, each essentially homogeneous and ideally suited by virtue of a great river system to become, as it did, a seat of world empire.

Palestine lay on the only natural road between Egypt with its Nile and the lands watered by the Tigris and Euphrates. Its population, which probably rarely if ever exceeded a million, was of distinctly mixed stock. For millennia Semitic seminomads from the vast Arabian desert had inter-

---

[6] It is to the sixth-century monk, Dionysius Exiguus, that we owe the custom of dating events by the birth of Jesus (B.C. and A.D.), no longer by the year of the founding of Rome (A.U.C.).

mittently pressed into what in contrast seemed a "land flow-
ing with milk and honey." Here they had mingled and
merged with those whom they found in possession of the
land—a populace made up in part of those who had earlier
made the same trek "from the desert to the sown," in part
of others of very different stocks who through the years had
come from the north and west, some for conquest, some in
quest of a land of refuge.

Hebrew and Jewish history was in large part shaped by
the land's experiences as an ancient Alsace-Lorraine, lying
between far more powerful neighbors. For a comparatively
short time little Israel, which had of necessity formed itself
by the union of tribes or clans (originally different, even if
genetically akin), first into a loose federation and then a
kingdom the better to withstand the opposition from those
already more firmly established in the land, had enjoyed a
semi-independent existence. This had been possible because
of the decline which had temporarily cramped the activities
of her far more powerful neighbors to the east and south.
This golden period soon passed but was never forgotten.
Instead, it became, as the years went by, more and more
idealized, the foretaste of what would once more be achieved
when their God saw his peculiarly beloved people ready for
their certain destiny.

After less than a century, the kingdom, which Saul and
David had established and Solomon had capitalized, split
into two parts—Israel to the north, Judah to the south—
which successively fell prey to the revived empires to the
east. The northern kingdom fell first, not because of its lesser
strength but because of its more exposed location and greater
value as plunder. Judah managed to maintain its existence
a century and a half longer, at the expense of very high tribute
and, at times, of virtual foreign control. Early in the sixth

century the final blow fell. The city of Jerusalem, with its all-important temple, which had recently come to be regarded as the one and only shrine where sacrifice to Yahweh [7] might be offered, was destroyed and the nation's back broken by the resulting deportations and captivity. From then on, save for the few years of independence, with Jewish kings —and a queen—once more on the throne, which resulted from the Maccabean revolt, Jewish history as an independent nation was over.

The days of Roman control, at least until the two disastrous and ill-starred rebellions in the century following the ministry of Jesus, were far less repressive than has often been popularly supposed. The story of growing Roman control in Asia Minor, Palestine, and east to the Euphrates has been often told, and need not be repeated here in detail. To one who views the story objectively and with candor it is hard to deny that the coming of Rome into the East was a blessing in disguise. To many ambitious petty princes, who had arisen as the earlier kingdoms had cracked and fallen, and who were engaged in constant boundary jumping and pillage, Rome's coming meant disaster. It was actually because

[7] There seems little justification for retaining the artificial spelling "Jehovah" for the Divine name. "Yahweh" is commonly regarded by scholars as the nearest equivalent in English of the original pronunciation. The form Jehovah is of late mediæval origin and is universally recognized as a sheer error. In the Hebrew Bible only consonants were written. Centuries later Jewish biblical scholars (Masoretes) inserted vowel points to facilitate pronunciation. Since for centuries the Divine name (commonly styled the *tetragrammaton* because of its four consonants) had been too sacred to be pronounced, it had become common practice to substitute, when reading, the other word, *Adonai* (Lord). This practice was naturally followed by the Masoretes, who used the vowels of *Adonai* with the consonants of the tetragrammaton to indicate that the word was to be pronounced *Adonai*. In the Middle Ages this was misunderstood and regarded as a single Hebrew word. Thus by combining the consonants of the one word with the vowels of the other the orthoëpic monstrosity "Jehovah" was produced.

one such territory in western Asia Minor—the kingdom of Pergamum—was willed to Rome by the dying king to prevent it from falling into the hands of ambitious and greedy neighbors, that Rome had taken, very reluctantly, this costly first step into the East.

The newly acquired territory, turned into the province of Asia, must be kept secure. That meant, as Rome had foreseen, many costly campaigns. The last pre-Christian century saw the gradual but steady expansion of the nation so amazingly competent in the orderly, if heavy-handed, administration of lands which for many years had known only insecurity and anarchy. Viewed from one side Rome's expansion meant the steady advance of Roman domination, with a series of new provinces and small semi-independent kingdoms, the latter with rulers who had learned, often by the hard way, the value of Roman friendship, the peril of her anger. But it meant more than this. It meant also security and peace, freedom to travel by land and sea, with far less danger from bandits and pirates. Admittedly "all roads led to Rome," but they were safeguarded by what thousands of grateful provincials gladly hailed, the *pax Romana*.

No clearer indication of the genuine gratitude for the blessing of the *pax Romana* can be found than in the emergence of what has come to be designated "emperor worship." Rome had done what local rulers had been unable to do. Tyranny and irresponsible and costly wars and banditry were over. Highways were open and safe for trade and travel. Earlier abuses by rapacious governors were effectually checked by Augustus and his immediate successors. Thus it is not surprising that, to people long accustomed to regard their rulers as of more than common clay, this amazing betterment could be explained only in terms of a divine genius, to whom glad tribute was but natural and proper:

"The birthday of God has brought to the world glad tidings. . . . From his birthday a new era begins."[8]

The rise of emperor worship was thus the natural expression of real appreciation—at times, even gratitude—not the invention of power-mad tyrants, as later Christians, with their inheritance from Judaism which forbade the worship of any save Yahweh, insisted. Emperor worship was not intended, and never regarded itself, as a substitute for other religions. It sought neither to replace them nor to quarrel with them. For a man in Asia or Bithynia to burn a bit of incense to *Roma*, later to the emperor, was essentially the same as an American raising his hat as the flag goes by or rising for the national anthem. The recognition of a new goddess Roma, the genius of the power which had brought order out of chaos, in no wise interfered with other loyalties. As the years went by and the earlier gratitude to Rome tended to lapse, it was not unnatural that the visible embodiment of the now increasingly abstract Roma—that is, the living emperor—tended more and more to come to the fore and to be associated gradually with the earlier local deities. In a word, the state cult did not owe its success to the destruction or decay of older religions; rather, it was the natural alliance with them that assured its triumph. And to the East, where for centuries their rulers had been considered divine, the apotheosis of dead rulers was not regarded as the way they *became* divine. On the contrary, it was the natural consequence of their already possessed divinity.

During the ministry of Jesus, little Palestine, too, was firmly held in the hand of Rome. It was a small but important part of the eastern frontier of the Roman empire. As such, Rome

[8] Dittenberger, *Orientis Græci Inscriptiones Selectæ* 458.

kept a watchful eye on what might easily become a danger spot. Almost exactly two centuries before the event echoed in the grim word, "crucified under Pontius Pilate," there had occurred the Maccabean rebellion. The little land of Palestine, long accustomed to foreign masters—Babylonia, Persia, and, since the death of Alexander the Great, first Egypt and subsequently Syria—found the demands of her then reigning master, Antiochus Epiphanes, intolerable. She succeeded in breaking away from the weakened and now moribund Greek kingdom of the Seleucids which, from the death of Alexander, had been her northern neighbor, and for thirty years her master.

During these many years of domination by outside powers —a constant source of tension and unrest, seeming such a contrast to their destiny as God's chosen people—they had been far from immune to the inroads of the different cultures, first Persian and then Greek, in which they were living. It was not a conscious borrowing. Every Jew was confident that he had God's complete revelation for him and his fellows in the unique book which God had given his especially beloved people through Moses and the prophets. Nevertheless, other ideas and ideals were to be met with on every hand, and during the centuries following the collapse of their kingdoms the Jews had not been able to remain unaffected.

Hopes for regained independence had not been realized. Instead they had become a dream for the future, when God, who was using these years of hardship and trial to perfect his beloved people—"their dross to consume, their gold to refine"—should find them ready for their glorious destiny. In consequence they had become essentially a religion instead of a nation. It had proved impossible to build city walls and establish a Jewish king upon David's throne; but there had been little or no attempt by her masters, either Persian or Greek, to prevent the practice and development of her folkways and beliefs. In a word, Judaism had become a church with a high priest at the head. With this change many alien ideas and even convictions had gradually come to be a part of what Judaism was confident was God's special revelation to her. Since no missionary coercion was upon them, the guard was down, and the well-nigh universal development, "first loathe, then pity, then embrace," took place.

Should foreign pressure be applied to compel ungodly and alien practices or to prevent those which God had ordained, then there would be a fight, regardless of the seeming odds. And in the year 168 B.C. the Seleucid king Antiochus Epiphanes provided just that spur. With his unwieldly kingdom crumbling, balked by Rome from gaining a foothold in Egypt, Syria's long-time deadly rival to the south, Epiphanes sought to achieve an impossible unity through his domain by forcibly blotting out alien cultures among his subject peoples.

That was the spark which set off the Maccabean rebellion. Sacrifice to their God forbidden, and to make it worse a hog sacrificed to a pagan deity on the all-holy temple altar; circumcision, God's especially designed symbol for his chosen people, forbidden; possession of a copy of the Torah, God's greatest gift to men and their blueprint for conduct, forbidden under penalty of death! Small wonder that this seemed the zero hour to the outraged Jews, horrified that even some of their brethren—and leaders—had proved themselves sons of the faithless Esau, ready to part with their birthright for the red pottage.

And the rebellion was amazingly successful. Within three years these religious restrictions were thrown off, and the

defiled altar was reconsecrated in triumph, still annually
celebrated in Hanukkah, the Feast of Lights. But more was
in store. Due to a combination of astute and able leadership, the death of the Syrian king and increasing confusion
and unrest in his crumbling domain, and great good luck,
the movement, which had started as a purely religious attempt to preserve God's revealed religion from extermina-
tion at the hands of uncircumcised gentiles, developed into
a successful bid for political freedom, unknown for more
than four centuries. In consequence, once again on David's
throne there sat a brief succession of Jewish kings. At first
this was hailed with joy, but as the years wore on this joy
was to turn into increasing unrest and discontent, for these
kings were also high priests. That spelled trouble. Nor is the
reason hard to see.

The rebellion had been sparked by an old priest, Mat-
tathias, and carried on by his sons. One of these, Jonathan,
who had succeeded his brother Judas as leader of the rebels,
had contrived to get himself appointed high priest. A little
later, at the time when real independence had been achieved,
Jonathan's brother and successor, Simon, had been enthusi-
astically confirmed in that office by the grateful people. This
was but natural, for after the fall of the southern kingdom in
586 B.C. there had long been no place for a Jewish king. In
consequence, the high priest, an office which historically
does not antedate the end of the kingdom, had gradually
become the head of what, as has been remarked, was essentially a church, not a state. With the triumph of the
Maccabean revolt, which had started solely in protest against
the Syrian attempt to prohibit Jewish religious practices, it
was natural that the leader should be acclaimed in the office
which had long been regarded as supreme.

But the successors of Simon wanted more. In their attempts once more to recreate a Jewish kingdom, through conquest of the territory which centuries earlier had been part of the domain of David, these ambitious high priests became kings as well as priests. At first this caused no undue concern. The destruction of the detested rival Samaritan temple, the conquest of the long-hated Edom (Idumea as it was now called), and the forcible Judaizing of the conquered territory—all this was acceptable to a people long oppressed but confident that the time of their triumph, while delayed, was sure.

As the years went by it became more and more evident that their rulers were no longer concerned with defending Jewish religion. Instead they were soldiers by profession. In consequence earlier enthusiasm waned and opposition became vocal. David, a man beloved by God and the ideal king, had not been permitted to build a temple because he was a soldier; yet here were men wearing the robes of the high priest whose arms were stained with blood to the elbows, constantly in the field leading foreign mercenary soldiers in costly and unnecessary military campaigns.

Thus gradually but surely there arose a deep-seated opposition to the royal house and, more important, to the view that this sort of military triumph was the glorious destiny for which the nation had long looked—and waited—in confident expectancy. So intense was the opposition to and hatred of the last of these high priest–kings, Alexander Jannæus, that a bitter civil war raged for years until finally crushed by the monarch, who celebrated his victory by crucifying many of the rebels and enjoying their dying agony as he lolled with his concubines in the temple of which he was God's high priest.

His widow ascended his throne after his death, and thus the dual office of high priest and monarch came of necessity to an end. This woman, Alexandra, very skillfully avoided the rebellion which would inevitably have followed the death of the loathed but dreaded Jannæus had his successor emulated Rehoboam's rash and tyrannical attempt to crush opposition after Solomon's death. While cannily keeping the power in her own hands, she made large concessions, especially to the group known as Pharisees, who had come to be regarded more and more as the religious leaders of the people. At her death, following a reign which in contrast to that of her hated husband came to be idealized in later memory, confusion again resulted, in which her two sons were involved as rivals for the rule.

It was at this moment that Rome intervened in the person of Pompey, who had brought to a successful conclusion the extended war against Mithradates of Pontus, who had sought to overrun all of Asia Minor, in which Rome had come to have large holdings and responsibilities. The little Jewish state which had sought to be an empire collapsed. All of her extra-Judean holdings, except Idumea, were stripped away, and she became a Roman possession.

The Seleucid kingdom, whose growing weakness had made possible the Maccabean rebellion and subsequent Jewish kingdom, was turned into a Roman province, the fourth of those created by Rome east of the Aegean Sea. Palestine —that is, the Jewish kingdom—appeared to Roman eyes properly a part of the territory to the north, i.e., Syria. At first it was intended to make all of Palestine a part of the new province.

This plan was subsequently modified, and one of Alexandra's sons was permitted by Rome to act as local governor of the tiny district about Jerusalem, from which the territories conquered and enslaved by the ambitious high priest–kings had been stripped away. Samaria and Galilee became a part of the province of Syria. The Greek cities of the seacoast and across the Jordan, gained at such a terrible price, were set free from the hated Jewish yoke, and many of them marked this date as the day of their freedom. The "freedom" entailed recognition of Rome's supremacy—it was freedom from Jewish sway—but to many it was a highly welcome contrast and relief. This was all in keeping with Rome's policy of a secure frontier and the preference, wherever practical, in minor but strategically important districts, for native rulers who understood local folkways, as the alien Roman did not, but who would find it to their advantage to be loyal to the city on the Tiber.

Behind the Hasmonean prince Hyrcanus, whom Pompey permitted to assume the rôle of ethnarch [9] in this new tiny part of the growing Roman frontier, was an astute Idumean, Antipater, who had been the chief adviser of both Alexander Jannæus and his widow Alexandra. It was he who had contrived that the unambitious and studious Hyrcanus, not the latter's ambitious and able brother, with whom he had been in contest at the time of Pompey's arrival, had gained Roman recognition.

During the following years Antipater made himself increasingly valuable in Roman eyes and succeeded eventually in having his son Herod appointed military governor of Galilee. Herod, true son of his father, improved his opportunity so well that eventually—at the insistence of Octavian and Antony—he was designated by the Roman senate king of Judea. And Herod made a reality out of what might at the moment seem scarcely more than a gesture. For thirty-seven years he ruled so effectively that Rome constantly added to his kingdom one territory after another, with the result that at his death his kingdom was larger—and more ably ruled—

[9] For the significance of this term see note 13.

than ever before in Hebrew history, even in the fabled days
of David and Solomon. The early years of Herod's rule were
during the death struggle of the old Roman republic which
culminated in the victory of Octavian, later known as Augustus, over Antony and the latter's source of undoing, Cleo-
patra. The last twenty-seven years of Herod's rule as a *rex
socius*—literally, "an allied king"—saw the birth and establishment of the Roman empire.

The Augustan age made the *pax Romana* a proverb. In
place of civil war and bloodshed, which had convulsed Rome
and all her holdings since the day of the fateful crossing of
the Rubicon by Augustus' uncle Julius, there was a time of
peace and prosperity. An amazingly effective form of government was contrived by Augustus, who had learned much
from the rise and fall of Julius. Skillfully avoiding the onus
of appearing a tyrant or dictator, he had surrendered all the
extensive authority granted him in the crisis culminating at
Actium, and had contrived for the Senate to give him back
the power which made him virtually master of the empire—
notably, complete control of all provinces which needed
military supervision, either because they were on open
frontiers or, because of local conditions, might prove danger
spots. In these "provinces of Cæsar," of which Syria was a
good example, the governor, with the title "proprætor," was
appointed by the emperor for an indefinite time and was
responsible solely to him.

Herod, who had received his title *rex socius* some years
before, while Octavian and Antony were still friends and
allies, was willingly continued by Augustus in the post he
had so ably filled. Herod knew on which side his bread was
buttered and continued to remain in the favor of his master.
In fact he was a little Augustus. As Augustus, so Herod. The
former had found Rome in brick and left it in marble; the

latter assiduously followed suit. The magnificent city of
Cæsarea, with its huge moles into the sea just south of
Carmel, was built to provide a respectable harbor, so manifestly wanting on the inhospitable Palestinian coast. The
temple in Jerusalem, which replaced the second temple,
built in the days after the exile, and which was a sorry substitute for the fabled temple of Solomon, symbolized the
efforts of this able but unpopular ruler. When started, it
was regarded with suspicion: it was a foul plot to raze the
temple. As work went on, the rumor was seen to be un-
founded. The workers were priests, trained as masons and
carpenters to guard the holy precincts from contamination
from tainted hands. And Herod himself was scrupulous never
to set foot in the temple he had made possible. Then over
the temple door he placed a Roman eagle! Reluctant gratitude was turned to instant fury, and an attempt to tear down
the hated symbol of servitude was made, only to end in the
execution of the leaders and deepened hatred of the Idumean
tool of Rome.

Despite his unpopularity and the evident joy that mocked
his magnificent funeral, Herod had been a very able ruler.
Palestine was in a far sounder condition than when, nearly
four decades earlier, he had returned from Rome with the
task of making his newly bestowed title, King, a reality. Outside the environs of Jerusalem, in those territories which the
Hasmonean kings, notably Alexander Jannæus, had overrun
and pillaged, and which Pompey had stripped away, but
which Augustus had from time to time added to Herod's
holdings, confident of his ability to administer them without recourse to arms, Herod's rule was far less offensive than
in Zion. Despite the unflattering verdict of the years—in no
small part due to the lurid stories, passed on gladly by
Josephus, of the family intrigues and resultant executions of

one son after another; and, especially in Christian eyes, of
the legend in Matthew of the brutal and senseless Slaughter
of the Innocents in Bethlehem, in which Herod repeats the
fruitless folly of the unnamed pharaoh in the days of that
other babe of promise, Moses—the impartial historian finds
it hard to deny that Herod had proved to be Israel's greatest
king.

His necessarily heavy hand, together with the fact that his
very presence was a constant daily reminder of their servitude to a foreign state, proved an added incentive to a group
of irreconcilable nationalists, who from the days of Rome's
first entry into the land had opposed the intruder and sought
to rally their countrymen to revolt. Josephus styles this group
"the fourth philosophy," [10] his colorless term to differentiate
them from the other three basic groups: Pharisees, Sadducees, and Essenes. Historians have commonly styled them
"zealots," a far from exact description, for actually the first
use of the term in this connection is by Josephus as a label
for one specific group of rebels who emerged in Jerusalem
during the bloody last days of the city's stand against Rome
during the rebellion of A.D. 66–73.[11] The basic attitude of
this group of firebrands—whether organized as a party or
"sect" is uncertain—is clear from their watchword: "The
sword, and not sparingly; no kings but Yahweh."

Many historians have seen their start in the interim of
unrest and bloodshed which followed Herod's death, while
the nation waited for Augustus' verdict as to its future.
Rather it seems wiser to see this as but one example of the
Jewish underground, which was so bitterly opposed to outside control. Surely they are to be seen in Hezekiah and his
Galilean followers whom Herod had suppressed when, as a
young man, he had gone to Galilee as a local governor.[12]

---

[10] Josephus, *Antt.* 18, 1, 6.   [11] Josephus, *Wars* 4, 3, 9.
[12] Josephus, *Wars* 1, 10, 4–8.

To be sure, Josephus characterized them as "robbers." The Jewish Sanhedrin, however, hostile to both Antipater and his son Herod, had sought to punish Herod for rooting these "robbers" from the land, whereas the Roman governor of Syria had heartily approved and had made the young Herod military governor of the whole district. All this suggests that the "robbers" had been, at least in their own eyes, loyal Jews set for the defense of their land against the foreign tyrant and his minions. We shall have to consider this group more in detail later, for they were to play an important part in the developing story. At the time of Herod's death they were a noisy minority, always a potential source of unrest and danger, but they had as yet failed to win the support of the more influential and soberer part of the nation.

When Herod's sons, whom he had nominated in his last will to be his successors, hastened to Rome for Augustus' verdict, a substantial group of Jews also went to beg that the will be disallowed and that the land become a part of the Roman province of Syria. Though often overlooked, this protest is highly significant. It surely suggests that the dream of a revived Jewish state, with a Jewish king on David's throne, was far from occupying the central place in Jewish thinking at this time that has often been accorded it. Instead it may well be pondered if the years of Herod's rule—he was a Jewish king despite his Idumean birth and Roman appointment—together with the bloodthirsty tyranny of the last of the Hasmonean kings, Alexander Jannæus, had not sickened many Jews of the whole notion of kings. It was not that Alexander was of the tribe of Levi, not Judah, and so no proper successor to David; nor that Herod was an Idumean, although joined by marriage to the Hasmonean nobility; rather, both of them had given the people all they could stand of kings, whatever their claims and whoever their sponsor might be.

Augustus ratified Herod's will with a few minor reserva-
tions, despite the pleas of the reluctant Jewish delegation
and the protest of one of the three sons (Antipas), who by
an earlier will had been nominated by Herod as his sole
successor. In consequence, Palestine was now divided into
three sections: Archelaus was confirmed as ethnarch of
Judea, Samaria, and Idumea; Antipas became tetrarch of
Galilee and the Peræa; their half-brother Philip, tetrarch of
the districts to the north and east of Galilee—Batanæa,
Trachonitis, and Auranitis—which through the years had
been added to Herod's territory by Augustus.[13] The latter
two sons remained in office for many years—well after the
crucifixion of Jesus—but Archelaus did not fare so well. In
less than a decade he was accused of gross mismanagement
by delegations of outraged Jews and Samaritans and was
summarily called to account by Augustus. His defense was
inadequate and he was removed from office and banished.

This clear evidence of unrest produced by mismanagement in a potential danger spot determined Augustus to
turn this ethnarchy into a province under direct rule from
Rome in the person of a procurator, as the governors of these
lesser imperial provinces were called. The governor of the
great province of Syria to the north, Quirinius, was entrusted
with the task of installing the new governor and of setting
up the machinery for enrolling the citizens as provincials
and for assessing the taxes. These steps, especially the census
—an echo of which is preserved in the familiar story in
Luke 2,[14] although the account there is seemingly mistakenly

---

[13] *Tetrarch* was the common Roman title for a native ruler, below the
rank of king, of a division of an Oriental country. *Ethnarch*, a similar but
somewhat more dignified title, which had been conferred by Julius Cæsar
upon Hyrcanus II, was conferred by Augustus on Archelaus, instead of
"king," as Herod's will had proposed.

[14] Luke 2:1-5.

dated a decade too early, while Herod was still alive—caused another outburst of rebellion. The ringleader was Judas of Galilee, who had been involved in the outbreak of violence which had drenched the land in blood ten years before, following Herod's death, while it was awaiting word from Rome as to its fate. The new rebellion was quickly and ruthlessly put down. Judas was slain, the census was taken, and the little Province of Judea was created, of which Pontius Pilate was to be for a decade the governor, and for two millennia the object of Christian hatred and scorn.

Thus, during the ministry of Jesus, dated as it is by the ominous word, "crucified under Pontius Pilate," little Palestine, now in three parts, like Caesar's "all Gaul"—two with native governors, the third a minor imperial province with a Roman governor residing in its capital city, Cæsarea—was firmly held in the hand of Rome. The reported words of the chief priests, "We have no king but Cæsar," [15] were literal and sombre fact.

This was their sorry fate, but the final chapter—a very different one—was yet to be written. God, their God, not Rome, was the real ruler and arbiter. He had promised; he would not, could not, go back on his word. This was the confidence of every Jew. The golden age was not in the past, despite their rosy and quite unhistorical memories of the good old days of David and Solomon, of Hezekiah and Josiah, of Queen Salome. Instead, it was still in the future, in the lap of their God, whose ways were not their ways, nor whose thoughts their thoughts, but who had chosen them as his own particular nation and who was preparing them for their coming and certain, if long delayed, glorious destiny.

Israel's confidence that she was uniquely God's chosen people was no new discovery. For centuries it had been a

[15] John 19:15.

fundamental conviction. The earliest national saga,[16] ante-
dating the Roman conquest by at least eight hundred years,
had established this confidence. The Deuteronomic reform,
with its easy optimism, "Do right; worship Yahweh aright,
and you will prosper," had given to it the added sanction of
Moses himself. Through the following centuries, despite the
scorn of an Amos, the uncomfortable and too easily disregarded insistence of the nameless prophet of the Exile as to
the obligations and responsibilities which such a unique
status involved, the vivid and so unprophetic paradigm of a
Jonah, this confidence had never waned. Instead, the confidence had continued, not abated but rather steadily developing and growing, that their choice as a unique and distinct people could only result in their eventual triumph.

The verdict of the years had been a sorry commentary
on that confidence. Jerusalem, which the Deuteronomists
knew could never fall, and which was, in consequence, the
only proper site for God's house and of all sacrifice, *did* fall.
The dreams of a restored monarchy under Zerubbabel, now
that the time of punishment was over, were rudely dashed.
Persia, Alexander, Egypt, Syria, now Rome—one after another, each of them had been seen and felt; still the confidence of the peculiar destiny of the peculiar people, whom
their God had chosen and with whom he had made a
covenant, did not lapse. Instead, Antæus-like, it grew the
stronger each time it was thrown to earth.

The insistence of the Deuteronomists: "Do right and you
will prosper; do wrong and you will be punished," when
grafted to the earlier confidence of God's solemn promise
of covenant, had enabled the feeble little nation to refuse to
bow to the common notion that a defeated people means a

---

[16] Commonly styled the "J document," one of the principal elements in
the early so-called "historical books" of the Hebrew Old Testament.

worsted God. Instead it had led such a religiously devout—
and politically astute—counselor as Jeremiah to the staggering insistence that, far from their God being worsted by
the more powerful gods of Assyria and Babylonia, it was
he that was using them to punish and to bring back to their
senses his beloved, but wayward and headstrong, people.
And on this confidence, now that the anticipated blow had
fallen, the prophet of the Exile (II Isaiah) put the capstone
of ethical monotheism: "There is no other God save our
God," and added weight to the explanation: "It is punishment for our sins; training for our destiny."

Thus through the years the confidence had grown: "Whom
the Lord loveth he chasteneth, and scourgeth every son
whom he receiveth." [17] It may well be that most theological
insights are the results of the experiences undergone—especially the sorry ones. And for Israel, with its deep-rooted
confidence that the God of the whole world was in a special
and unique sense the Lord God of Israel, only so could the
long and sorry chapter of its history be understood.

God was perfecting them, cleansing them of their sins,
burning away their dross, refining the gold. So the woes were
explained: dispersion of many of the faithful from Zion; the
nation in bondage to one heathen power after another. It
was not due to weakness, theirs or their God's; rather it was
but part of their training for their coming glorious destiny.
When their God saw that they were ready, then the glorious
day of promised destiny would dawn. Their triumph would
be evident to all. Israel's enemies, who had thought that it
was by their own arms and armor that they had triumphed,
would be bitterly and rudely disillusioned.[18]

---

[17] The paraphrase in Hebr. 12:6 of Prov. 3:12.
[18] For one of many such expressions of conviction see Isa. 10:5–34.

2

"The things concerning Jesus"

AND HE OPENED the book, and found the place where it was written:

The Spirit of the Lord is upon me,
Because he anointed me to preach good tidings to the
    poor:
He hath sent me to proclaim release to the captives,
And recovering of sight to the blind,
To set at liberty them that are bruised,
To proclaim the acceptable year of the Lord.

And he closed the book, and gave it back to the attendant, and sat down: and the eyes of all in the synagogue were fastened on him. And he began to say unto them, To-day hath this scripture been fulfilled in your ears." [1]

"The time is fulfilled, and the kingdom of God is at hand: repent ye, and believe in this good news." [2]

"And the common people heard him gladly." [3]

"... this man, if he were a prophet...." [4]

"Is not this the carpenter, the son of Mary...?" [5]

[1] Luke 4:17–21.   [2] Mark 1:15.   [3] Mark 12:37.
[4] Luke 7:39.   [5] Mark 6:3.

"Now the chief priests and the whole council sought witness against Jesus to put him to death; and found it not." [6]

"And Pilate, wishing to content the multitude, released unto them Barabbas, and delivered Jesus, when he had scourged him, to be crucified." [7]

It is scarcely an overstatement or undue simplification to say that in these few short passages stand revealed the basic facts in the story of a life which in veriest truth was destined to "sway the future." And these facts, when set down simply, are: a man completely convinced that God had revealed to him that at long last the promised time of triumph was at hand, the period of testing and trial was momentarily to pass, the new age to dawn. Convinced himself, he was able to convince others, and they gladly harkened. To those in positions of authority and power the man and his message were alike an outrage and a menace and had to be suppressed at any cost. And with little difficulty they were able to convince the resident governor of the necessity of quenching the blaze before it was too late.

Of the birth and early years of Jesus we have no reliable information. The earliest of our gospels, Mark, introduces him as a mature man as he began his task of preaching the cataclysmic end of the present age and the dawn of the new. In Matthew and Luke are accounts of his birth at Bethlehem, the son of a mother who had conceived him in consequence of having been "overshadowed by the power of the Most High." [8] The stories differ widely in detail, and when viewed alone are liable to most unfortunate distortion.

To readers whose knowledge of the ancient past is not

[6] Mark 14:55.   [7] Mark 15:15.
[8] Matt. 1:18–2:12; Luke 1:26–2:20.

restricted to the gospels they provide no especial problem. They are far from unique or even surprising. Precisely the same basic story is to be found in the case of many heroes who had achieved fame in the past, as Romulus, the elder Scipio, Augustus, Sargon, Cyrus, Alexander the Great, Pythagoras, and Plato. It was as natural to the ancient world to explain unusual prowess or achievement as due to a divine parent as it is to us to style one superlatively great of "more than human clay." The chaste and exquisite manner in which the gospel accounts are phrased makes them a lovely part of the Christian tradition. The stories themselves, told rather less than a century after his death, attest the impress he had made. "Though dead he yet speaketh." It is one of the unfortunate results of mistaken piety to deprive them of their eternal charm and true historic value by treating them as staid and unimaginative prose, with the inevitable results that in the eyes of some the dignity of human birth must suffer, in the eyes of others the early, cruel Jewish burlesque of the story may well seem true.[9] Of the other charming story, the visit of the twelve-year-old boy to the temple, much the same must be said.[10] It has become a part of the heritage from the past, another bit of later appreciation of the one whose presence made their "hearts burn within them." Of course one such as he must have shown his divine precocity, as had so regularly those whose later years were crowned with greatness.[11]

[9] The occasional references to the bastard son of the Roman soldier Panthera and Mary, which are to be found in Celsus (Origen, *Against Celsus* i, 28 and 32) and the Talmud and the *Toledoth Jeschu* (cf. Eisenmenger, *Entdecktes Judenthum*) are the not unnatural retort of those by whom the early Christian insistence that Joseph was not the father of Jesus was accepted, but not with the contingent Christian explanation.

[10] Luke 2:41–52.

[11] For a fuller discussion of the birth stories and of the story of the twelve-year-old Jesus, see my articles, "The Christian Stories of the

With confidence we must ascribe his birth, as well as early years, to the little Galilean town of Nazareth. The fact that all the gospels make reference to it as the town from which he came awakens confidence, for this is precisely the sort of detail which later imaginations would not have conjured up. The year of his birth is unknown. That he was crucified by Pontius Pilate, whose term of office was A.D. 26–36, is certain. While Luke's reference to the "fifteenth year" of Tiberius Cæsar is in connection with the preaching of John the Baptist,[12] it would seem probable that he meant it to serve as the date of that one's greater successor. Thus A.D. 28 would seem to be indicated. The common assumption that Jesus was then thirty years of age is far from certain. To be sure, this would seem to be the meaning of Luke's singularly obscure word, which so perplexed subsequent copyists and translators: "And Jesus himself, when he began to teach, was about thirty years of age."[13] Whether this rests on definite tradition or is simply an inference from Old Testament stories, in which this was the common age for beginning service,[14] is at best uncertain.

To some this date of A.D. 28 has seemed buttressed by the reference to Herod the Great in Matthew's birth story. Since Herod died in 4 B.C., it has been assumed that Jesus was born shortly prior to that date. But this assumption is quite unwarranted. The story of the Slaughter of the Innocents[15] is unknown save in the Matthæan saga. Its absence from

Nativity" (*Journal of Biblical Literature,* LIX, 3 [Sept., 1940], pp. 317–338) and "Along Highways and Byways" (*Harvard Theological Review,* XLIV, 2 [April, 1951], pp. 67–92).

[12] Luke 3:1. [13] Luke 3:23.

[14] Cf. "And Joseph was thirty years old when he stood before Pharaoh" (Gen. 41:46); "David was thirty years old when he began to reign" (II Sam. 5:4).

[15] Matt. 2:16–18.

Josephus, if an actual deed of Herod, is unexplainable. The fact that the story itself is so completely parallel to the classic tale of Moses' providential escape from the wicked pharaoh [16] —and in a book where Jesus is so consciously depicted as Moses' greater successor—does not incline the historian to accept it as authentic history. And much the same must be said for the census made "when Quirinius was governor of Syria." By attempting to link this Lucan story with the Matthæan, this well-known census has been forced back into the days of Herod against all historical evidence and probability. Instead, it certainly took place at the time of the unseating of Herod's son Archelaus and the formation of the Province of Judea (A.D. 6).

Nor is there any real evidence as to the length of the ministry. The still occasionally repeated "three years" is due solely to the Gospel of John, which records several visits of Jesus to Jerusalem to attend passover feasts. This gospel is invaluable for an understanding of later thinking about Jesus. It is worthless so far as chronology is concerned. The other three gospels—which means in essence Mark, repeated by Matthew and Luke—give no indication at all of the length of his public career. Their failure to record any visits to Jerusalem prior to the fatal one has frequently been interpreted to indicate a brief activity. Actually, the nature of his message and the probability that it could not go long unchecked would seem a more sure basis for the likelihood of but a short public career. Much the same must be said for the locale of the ministry. In the Markan outline, substantially reproduced by Matthew and Luke, it is restricted to Galilee and nearby districts until the fatal trip to Jerusalem. The fact that heralding his dangerous word about the impending end of the age and society—that is, the upsetting of the

[16] Exod. 1:15–2:10.

status quo—would not likely go long unchecked in Jerusalem would seem to make this Markan setting of the ministry not improbable, and Jesus' first visit to Jerusalem his last.

In view of our complete lack of information about Jesus until he appears, without explanation, in the gospel pages as the flaming herald of the impending new age, the query is not unnatural: "What started him? What led one who had hitherto been a Galilean carpenter to assume the rôle of a prophet of God?" for there can be but little question that thus he regarded himself and was regarded by those to whom he spoke.

To many this is no question at all; or rather, the answer to it is obvious: "God did it." To those who see these now distant years as a part of history where results have causes, this glib answer, with its portentous "in the fullness of time," is no answer at all, but simply resolves into the companion query, "How did God do it?" For what they know of history seems so clearly to reveal that in this orderly universe we have an equally orderly God who works through human hearts and minds and speaks through human voices. The earlier off-stage voice, with its repeated "Let it be done," no longer seems an explanation but rather a bid to further search.

An answer increasingly common has been found in a fancied relation between Jesus and the enigmatic John the Baptist. At the moment, due to loudly heralded discoveries in the cliffs along the Dead Sea and a welter of confident, but far from harmonious, explanations and pronouncements about them—not unsuggestive of a pyramid balanced upon its apex—this relation has been restressed and reinterpreted with rather more zeal than caution.

All four of the gospels begin with a brief account of John

the Baptist and the baptism at his hands of Jesus.[17] To many
this has seemed the complete explanation to our earlier question. It was the activity of this spectacular wilderness
preacher which started the carpenter from Nazareth on his
career. And quite despite the fact that the several gospel accounts would seem to contradict it, it has been increasingly
common to see Jesus as a disciple of the Baptist until the
latter's arrest at the hands of Herod Antipas, the native governor (tetrarch) of Galilee and the Perea. Only then did
Jesus start on his own and with a message suggested by his
earlier preceptor, if modified and developed as the days of
independent activity went on.

That this reading of the story is correct appears to me far
from certain or even probable. To me the evidence points
in the opposite direction. Instead of the modern hypothesis
that Jesus was a disciple of John, thereby accounting for
some elements of similarity between their messages, I should
be inclined to suggest that the two movements were originally quite unrelated, but that subsequently Christians had
sought to bring a later generation of followers of the Baptist
into their ranks by the claim that John had been but the
conscious forerunner of their crucified Lord and that his one
function had been to designate his greater successor. Not
only would this serve to minimize rivalry—traces of which
are still to be seen even in the rewritten accounts—between
the two groups, and to swell their (Christian) ranks, but by
identifying John as Elijah *redivivus* Christians would have a
powerful answer to the Jewish claim that "the great and
terrible day of the Lord," whose imminent approach they
were now heralding, as had their crucified Lord, could not
be at hand without the advent of Elijah.[18] The answer was

[17] In John it is implied but not described or even explicitly asserted
(1:29–36).
[18] Mal. 4:5.

now easy. Elijah had come, as predicted, and had met his fate at the hands of a second more deadly and successful Jezebel.

In addition, this hypothesis, unlike its rival, meets and provides a reasonable answer to the queries: Why the complete silence in the gospels about baptism? Why its comparatively late appearance as a part of Christian practice? These questions are insistent. The one element with regard to the activity of John in which both the gospels and Josephus agree is the rite of baptism. Had Jesus been baptized by John—not to mention had he been, even for a short time, his disciple—it is far from easy to give a satisfactory answer to the question: Why, then, did Jesus seemingly ignore the rite which, according to the gospel stories, had apparently been such a significant experience for him? Why the constant contrast between the baptism in water which John practised and the very different baptism in spirit (and fire) which his successor was to bestow? [19] And all of this is heightened by the fact that, at the time our gospels were framed, water baptism was the invariable requirement for membership in the Christian group. Thus there would certainly seem little reason for suppressing mention of the rite had it been a part of Jesus' activity.

Nor is the objection valid that the story of Jesus' own baptism at the hands of John is historically certain because of its very awkwardness—why should *he* undergo baptism? Rather, once baptism had become the universal symbol, or sacrament, it was read further and further back into the history, as is invariably the case in a religion that takes itself seriously as a religion of revelation. What is now under the blessing of God must always have so been. Furthermore, just as Jesus had himself commanded its use in his final Great Commission, which a later writer puts in his mouth as a

[19] Mark 1:8; Matt. 3:11; Luke 3:16; Acts 1:5.

prelude to and guarantee of the coming gentile mission, so Jesus himself had consecrated it for all time by his own example.

Thus it would seem entirely possible to explain the presence of stories of the momentary contact of Jesus with John as the product of later Christian thought and practice. Similarities in the messages of the two leaders, which now are to be seen in the Christian gospels, would seem more plausibly to be explained as due to John, once he had been brought into the Christian picture, having been provided with a "Christian" message, than that he had been the source of Jesus' words. The other difficulty in the traditional picture, the proclamation by John of the advent of a greater successor (which if historical, Josephus so strangely omits, and which has always embarrassed interpreters hard put to explain the seeming disillusion which John evidences in the query he later raised),[20] may for the moment be reserved for later consideration,[21] but with the real likelihood that it too is but one of Jesus' own words which his later followers had come to find more convenient to place in the mouth of another.

[20] Matt. 11:3; Luke 7:19.

[21] For a fuller discussion of the revision of stories about John and of his subordination to Jesus, see my article, "Once Again: John the Baptist," in *Religion in Life*, XXVII, 4 (Autumn, 1958), pp. 557–566.

3

"The times of refreshing"

Whiле iт is impossible at this remove to postulate the precise incident or circumstance which led Jesus to
exchange the carpenter's bench for the thankless rôle of a
prophet of God,[1] the larger occasion for the choice appears
to me clear. He had become convinced that the long-
expected fulfillment of God's promise of old was immediately
to be realized; and he had also become convinced that he,
Jesus, had been selected by God as his prophet to announce
this fact.

It has been common through the years to recognize that
for Judaism, unlike many religions for which the golden age
lay in the past, the best was yet to be. God had chosen this
people as his especial beloved; in them his destiny was in a
very real sense involved. By a solemn covenant he had bound
them to him. Their religion was destined to be the religion
of the world. What was believed to have been the promise to
Abraham, undisputed and unending possession of the land
of Canaan, was never forgotten; indeed it remains the explanation of modern Zionism. As the years went by and as

[1] See pp. 83 f. for further discussion of this matter.

45

the experiences through which the nation passed had resulted in changes, both political and religious, among which none could compare with the growth and development of the tribal god Yahweh into the one and only God of the world, there were also changes in the way this glorious future was being viewed.

The successive fall of the northern and southern kingdoms and the resultant Babylonian captivity constitute a real watershed in Jewish thinking. The eighth-century prophets —Amos, Hosea, Micah—had been vindicated. Their warning of sure disaster had been realized. Almost overnight the tone of the preaching changes. The nation had indeed fallen because of its sin, its flouting the demands of its God. Now that disaster had come a new note is constantly heard: restoration and a new start. "Comfort ye, comfort ye my people" [2] does not replace but is added to the stark warnings and unqualified predictions of doom which had earlier been the incessant word of the watchmen in Israel. It is not that the prophets of the Exile and their successors deny Israel's guilt. But whereas their predecessors had been concerned with it and it alone, the later prophets not unnaturally, now that the blow has fallen, see a break in the clouds and the presage of a new and more glorious destiny. Total and final destruction of the nation cannot be the purpose of God. If so, what about his earlier promises? This problem had not been faced by the earlier prophets. Their successors could not escape it, and in wrestling with it they found an answer. Purged of her sins, a purified Israel could look forward to restoration.

Thus the fall of Babylon before Cyrus seemed to many, as it did to the nameless prophet of the Exile, the direct act of their God, for the express purpose of restoring the

[2] Isa. 40:1.

errant but now humbled nation and of making clear to their
enemies that it was he, not they, who had brought Israel low.
In those days following the Exile, when, due to Persia's policy
of permitting her captive peoples to return to their home-
lands, they were once more in Jerusalem and its environs,
there can be but little question that the vision of a restored
throne of David came to the fore. But these hopes, furthered
by Haggai and Zechariah, were speedily dashed. It soon
became evident to all that the earlier dream that the success
of Cyrus was solely for the purpose of destroying their Babylonian captors and restoring the Jewish nation was far
from true.[3] Persia permitted them to build a temple, but
restored city walls were quite another matter. Zerubbabel,
of the seed of David and an aspirant for the throne of his
fathers, fades from the picture. In his stead stands Joshua the
high priest. In a word, instead of a nation with a king on its
throne, there emerges, as we have seen, a church with a
priest at its head.

During the two centuries of Persian control the expected
restoration under a "scion of David" slipped more and more
into the background. Many found their condition quite bear-
able. True, political independence was impossible, but a
complete religious freedom was theirs. An attitude of let-
well-enough-alone became increasingly the order of the day,
not only for those in authority—the priestly ring and their
supporters, who in the days of Jesus' ministry were to be
seen in the wealthy and politically astute Sadducees—but
also for the increasingly influential group who, as the years
had passed, had come to be the religious mentors of the
nation and whom we know as the Pharisees.

The Maccabean rebellion, which had been at its start a
purely religious protest against what had seemed the attempt

[3] For an expression of this confidence see Ezra 1:1–4.

by Antiochus Epiphanes to blot out true worship, had not
only been successful, but due to many factors—chief among
which was the growing weakness of the Seleucid kingdom,
which from the days of Antiochus the Great (*ca.* 198 B.C.)
had held sway over the little land—had actually ended in
a short period of political independence, with high priests,
bearing the title king, engaged in wars of conquest and pillage.

Rome had brought to a close this chapter, the last in which
a Jewish king was actually such in his own right. Later, as
we have seen, Herod might sit upon the throne of David,
but he sat there because Rome had seen fit there to seat him.
And during these years, in which once again there had been
a king, increasing opposition and hostility to him had been
the order of the day. The brutality and ruthlessness of the
bloodthirsty high priest–king Alexander Jannæus, the absolute domination by the hated puppet Herod—this had
caused, in the thinking of many, significant changes in the
dream of the coming age of gold.

Actually, in the early days of the new Roman Province
of Judea the little land had far more real freedom to manage
its own affairs than it had had during the days when a king
sat on the throne. Domination by Rome was, to be sure, an
outrage, but it was a part of God's inscrutable plan for their
future. Centuries of domination by foreign overlords had
left their mark. For many it made little difference who was
in control. For the religious leaders, largely to be found in
the ranks of the Pharisees during the ministry of Jesus, the
great imperative was devotion to the law, that is, to the
Scriptures, in which God's complete will and purpose was
to be found. With this went a tendency to remain aloof from
matters political. When God saw fit to intervene, saw that
the nation was ready for its coming glorious destiny—what-

ever its precise form was to be—he would act. In the interim
they were to make themselves ready. For those, like the
chief-priestly families and the Sadducees, who in their control of the great and powerful Sanhedrin occupied a position
of power never enjoyed while kings like Jannæus or Herod
held sway, any thought of violent change was anathema. Well
did they know the certain consequences of such folly. And
the tragedy which resulted a few years later—the temple
destroyed, Jerusalem in ruins—when the people took the bit
in their teeth and raced into conflict with Rome, proved
their astuteness.

To others, commonly styled the Home Rule group, hundred per cent nationalists, this apathy and indifference
seemed outrageous. "The sword, and not sparingly; no king
but Yahweh" was their watchword, and their aim was to
force the nation to take the fatal step of rebellion. Would
they so do, God would instantly rally to their defense as
he had in the past. As in the days of Joshua and Gideon,
let the pitchers be broken and the lamps revealed, and victory would be theirs. Was not one man with Yahweh more
than equal to a thousand?

As we have seen, this attitude was nothing new. From the
days of Rome's advent it had been present. That during the
days of Jesus' ministry these views were shared by the majority is most unlikely. Nonetheless these perfervid nationalists constituted a problem to be reckoned with, and their
presence is to be seen in occasional references in the gospels,
notably in the malicious question propounded to Jesus by
his opponents with regard to the payment of tribute to
Rome.[4]

Thus the general features of what may be inexactly styled
the "peculiarly Jewish" hopes for the coming golden age

[4] Mark 12:14 ff.; Matt. 22:17 ff.; Luke 20:22 ff.

are clear. It would be in the future, it would be on this earth.
It would ensure the universal recognition of the sole sovereignty of God. Would it be the consequence of the final
conversion of the gentiles, and dawn when the last unbeliever
saw the light? Would it be the consequence of a dramatic
intervention of God, who would blast all opposition from
the earth? Opinions differed, as the proverbial alternative
showed: The Messiah, son of David, will come only in a
generation that is wholly worthy or in one that is wholly
unworthy.[5] All were agreed that when the day dawned God
would be worshipped by all mankind. Thus, reduced to
lowest terms, this hoped-for golden age would mean the
universally recognized reign of Israel's God, on this earth,
in the future. For some it would be in terms of a political
restoration, with the throne restored and a Jewish king—a
second David, perchance a second Hezekiah—upon it. For
others it would be a purely theocratic rule, in which in a
very literal sense God would be "all in all."

But in contrast to these "purely Jewish" expectations there
was to be found a very different range of ideas. Instead of
the golden age—that is, the burgeoning to supremacy of
Israel, her God and her religion—this other line of thought
looked for the cataclysmic dawn of the Age to Come.

The source of the basic elements of this quite different
view of the future is with most probability to be seen in
Iranian, not Jewish, thinking, although at the time of the
Christian beginnings this view had been adopted, if not
thought through, by many a Jew. During the two centuries
of Persian control these ideas had been in the air, and since
their Persian masters seem never to have sought forcibly to
impress them, to many a Jew, who would have been scandalized at the thought of adopting under pressure—or bor-

[5] Sanhedrin 98a.

rowing—heathen ideas, they had gradually become part of his heritage.

The Iranian or Persian concept was: In the future a great cataclysm would take place, which would bring the present evil age to a close. In a very literal sense it would be the end of the world, for the world would be consumed by fire to purge it of all evil. Out of the ashes of the old would emerge a new and glorious world in which the righteous would take their place. This would mark the end of the twelve-thousand-year struggle between Ahriman (Angra Mainyu) and his hosts of evil and Ormuzd (Ahura Mazda) and his angels of light. Shaoshyant, the last of the three Iranian saviors, would be the agent who prepared men for the new age, the rousing of the dead, the setting up of the final judgment, and the settling of men's fates.

Traces of this type of thought, commonly styled apocalyptic, are to be seen in the writings of the postexilic prophets: the approaching world catastrophe in Isaiah 24–27, the series of ecstatic visions in Ezekiel 40–48, the visions and imagery of the latter half of the book of Zechariah. But this sort of thinking comes to full bloom in a series of books which appeared during a period of almost exactly three centuries, ushered in by the Maccabean uprising and concluded by the awful reprisals which followed the ill-starred rebellion against Rome led by Bar Cochba in the days of Hadrian in the early second century.

In the most literal sense these books may be called a literature of crisis. They all breathe a bitter and passionate hatred of this world in which the righteous are in sore affliction and must be so long as the present evil order lasts. But they are far from being a literature of despair. On the contrary, they are tocsins of the most extravagant hope, and are intended to rouse their readers to fresh courage and confidence. The zero hour has struck; the last hellish onslaught is under way. This proves that the final victory is at hand. "A few more marchings weary; then we'll gather home."

This is the note dominant in all these writings, be it Daniel, with its passionate hatred of the Seleucid kingdom, written during the bloody first days of the Maccabees, or the book of Revelation, which now stands at the end of our New Testament, but with the same passionate hatred of Rome, the then present tyrant. Mistaken attempts to turn these ultrapractical calls to arms against a very present foe in the author's own day, whose immediate doom is certain, into timetables of a series of century-distant—often millennium-distant—coming events have led to many most unfortunate consequences.

One reason which has so often led to a mistaken idea of the nature of these hopes is that it was the regular practice of the author to ascribe his writing to some hero of the distant past—Daniel, Ezra, Moses, Abraham, even Adam—who thus "prophesied," that is, foretold what was destined to come to pass. The important point to remember is that the actual author was convinced that he himself stood at the very end of all history. The bell had sounded. In the very immediate future the long-expected day would dawn. Thus *for him* the real future to be foretold was very brief. But since he is writing in the name of a long-dead hero of the past, he makes that figure foretell the long period from *his* day to the present. In a word, these writings are regularly a compound of a review of the *history* from the date of the purported author to the time of the actual writer, plus the latter's own confident foretelling of the short period yet in store.

The book of Daniel set the pace for this type of writing. In the series of visions which this ancient worthy saw of what was transpiring in heaven—and which thus is reflected on earth, for the one determines the other in this type of writing—the history of Israel, culminating in the Maccabean struggle, is crystal-clear. Three beasts appear; then a fourth before whom the first three fall. On the head of the fourth beast is a horn in which are "eyes like the eyes of a man, and a mouth speaking great things." The heavens are opened. God, worshipped by a vast angelic host, is seen. Judgment is set, and Israel, seen as a human being (literally a "son of man")—in contradistinction to the doomed, awesome beasts representing Babylon, Media, Persia, and Greece—appears before the Ancient of Days and receives an "everlasting dominion, which shall not pass away."

Due in no small part to the influence of Daniel, which did much toward popularizing these notions of the impending dawn of the new age to come, the colorless term "son of man," which in the Semitic idiom simply meant "man," in the sense of the Latin *homo,* came apparently to be used as a distinctive title—"the Man"—for the supernatural figure (Shaoshyant) who was destined to come to set up and preside over the coming final judgment.

In this type of thought, commonly called apocalyptic, and in the literature it produced is thus to be seen a very real difference in outlook from what I have called "purely Jewish" expectations for the future. Instead of the hope of a good time coming in the providence of God, when Israel, now scourged of her sins, would be deemed ready and worthy of the glorious destiny which had been long promised, there is to be a supernatural deliverance accomplished by the cataclysmic advent of the new age, that is, the Age to Come, with a final judgment inaugurated by a specially-sent supernatural angelic agent.

To what extent these two, so basically different, types of thinking had come to be confused and combined in popular circles by the time of the ministry of Jesus, is impossible to say. It is far from improbable that in the thinking of some the dream of the good time coming should be made to coincide with the advent of the cataclysmic Age to Come; that the future Davidic king, if he chanced to be in the picture, should tend to be transplanted into the apocalyptic new age and, losing his function of destroying Israel's enemies in war, should gain the more cosmic function of destroying evil and acting as final judge—in a word, that "son of David" and "Son of man" should come to be identified.

That all this is possible is not to be denied. But "possibility" and "certainty" are far from synonymous, much unguarded writing about "messianic expectations" to the contrary notwithstanding. We have no real evidence that these identifications had actually been made *in Judaism* before the ministry and death of Jesus. In the early decades of Christian thinking they were made; for early Christians in their zeal for explaining the significance of their crucified leader came to identify him with both of these figures. Thus, by seemingly good mathematics, things equal to the same thing are equal to each other.

Not dissimilarly, in later Jewish (non-Christian) thinking a harmonization of the two sets of views was attempted in the apocryphon known as IV Ezra. In this writing the time is seen approaching when the Anointed, that is, the Davidic king of Israel, will appear, will destroy all opposition, and will reign for four hundred years. Then he and all mankind will die—"My son, the anointed one, will die." [6] This will mark the end of "this age." Then will come the Resurrection and the Final Judgment, the dawn of the Age to Come.

That these or similar harmonizations and accommodations had been reached in the "fifteenth year of Tiberius" is most

[6] IV Ezra 7:29.

uncertain. In addition, it is unlikely that by that time the word *anointed* (in Hebrew, *mashiah*) had come to be the title of one specific figure, namely, the future Davidic king. In the Old Testament and in the Apocrypha the word is not a noun, that is, the descriptive term applied to any one specific figure destined to appear in the future for any definite purpose. Rather, it is an adjective, and as such is applied variously to kings, high priests, patriarchs, even to Cyrus. Thus, in essence, it connoted *designated, appointed, consecrated, honored* by the Lord for whatever function he was to perform. In a word, Jesus, as any other pious Jew, might well have considered himself "anointed by the Lord"—much as in our churchly idiom we say a man is "called of God"—but with no thought of thereby laying claim to be the Davidic king for whose coming a later generation, after the fall of Jerusalem and crushed by the heavy reprisals exacted by Rome in penalty for the rebellion, looked with passionate hope.

It is unfortunate that through the years it has been common practice to use the phrase "the Messianic hope" to describe the expectation of future blessedness to which all pious Jews looked forward. The *Messianic* hope should connote the age in which the Messiah was to appear, whereas in fact it was to the age—not for the party who was to bring it in—that Israel looked. In large blocks of Jewish thinking, as has been already remarked, there was no emphasis upon a specific figure. *The* Messianic hope cannot fail to suggest that there was *one* expectation which all the pious held. Instead, there was no field where a greater amount of latitude for individual opinions prevailed.

But despite the absence of one definite, charted expectation for the future; despite the fact that for different men there were different minds, and that in the course of the years

of enforced waiting there had been many developments and
decided changes, first in one direction, then in another;
despite the undoubted fact that for many then, as now, involved in the daily round of wresting a living and keeping
soul and body together, there was little time for pondering
the precise nature of the coming change—nonetheless in
every Jew, be he a peasant, or fisherman by Galilee's shore,
or a priest in fabled Zion, was the steadying confidence that
he was not alone, but was part of a people guarded and
cherished by the Lord God of hosts; that it was he, not their
captors, who was directing the affairs of men; that in the
perplexing book of life the last chapter—and a singularly
glorious one—was yet to be written.

4

"A prophet mighty in deed and word"

A<small>ND SOME BEGAN</small> to spit on him, and to cover his face, and to buffet him, and to say unto him, Prophesy: and the officers received him with blows of their hands." [1] In this horrid picture, made all the more sickening by its stark brevity, is to be seen a very important detail, almost certainly primitive and untouched, which the student, anxious to gain a firsthand picture of how Jesus appeared to his hearers, may well ponder. It is the terse and mocking word, "Prophesy." Both Matthew and Luke repeat this Markan word, with brief additions to give it force to their readers. The former expands: "Prophesy unto us, thou Christ: who is he that struck thee?" [2] Luke repeats, but without the words, "thou Christ." [3]

At once the query arises: why in their brutal horseplay did the rabble indulge in the sneering taunt, "Prophesy"? The most likely answer is the simple and obvious one. This was the role in which Jesus had appeared: a prophet. In all

[1] Mark 14:65. [2] Matt. 26:68. [3] Luke 22:64.

57

likelihood this earliest appraisal of him was the natural consequence of his own unqualified claim.

In the years following the crucifixion, as has already been
suggested, title after title came to be applied to him as his
followers sought to answer the question: "Who then was he?"
But that the identification of him as a prophet is to be seen
as one of these later accolades is most improbable. Instead,
the tendency appears to have been in precisely the opposite
direction—namely, to minimize, without flatly denying, this
estimate and to substitute for it others which seemed more
significant and worthy. Thus in Peter's speech, on the first
Pentecost we have: "Let all the house of Israel therefore
know assuredly, that God hath made him both *Lord* and
Christ, this Jesus whom ye crucified." [4] Despite the deft
touches with which the gifted author has made this speech
sound primitive, it is most unlikely that these identifications
had been made at so early a date.

The tendency, early at work, is seen in full flower in what
seems to the modern reader an amazing, if not shocking,
word attributed to Jesus in the second-century apocryphal
writing known as *The Epistle of the Apostles.* In this writing
Jesus is represented as talking with his disciples in the interim between his crucifixion and ascension. Among other
things he mentions his birth. It was he, Jesus, who had appeared to Mary in the form of the angel Gabriel and had
formed himself and entered her body: "for I alone was a
minister unto myself in that which concerned Mary." [5]

This is no esoteric speculation, although it has frequently
been so regarded. Rather it is the logical, if grotesque and
to us repellent, result of the growing unwillingness, so clear
if restrained, in the Gospel of John, of allowing any one—
his mother [6] or his brothers [7] or any others [8]—to minister

[4] Acts 2:36.   [5] *Epistle of the Apostles* 14.
[6] John 2:4 ff.   [7] John 7:2–10.   [8] John 2:25.

to or aid or advise him. Thus more and more what may
properly be styled the earliest view—a prophet sent by God
to announce the impending change and endued for his task
with God's own spirit, which enabled him to perform his task
—tended to drop into the background. Instead arose the
seemingly more adequate explanation: he did what he did,
because he was what he was.[9]

Editors may revise manuscripts, but they generally leave
by inadvertence a revealing clue. Thus in our gospels, although they show the clearest evidence of long development,
are yet to be found most revealing touches. In addition to
the word of his callous hecklers, "Prophesy," are other
glimpses of the same earlier outlook.

In the Lucan story of the anointing of Jesus by the sinful
woman,[10] whose love and contrition were so tenderly re-
warded—a story which must be regarded as Luke's own
lovely revision of the Markan story of the anointing of Jesus
just prior to the final tragedy [11]—stands the revealing word
of the Pharisee, who is Jesus' host at dinner: "This man,
if he were a prophet, would have perceived who and what
manner of woman this is that toucheth him, that she is a
sinner." Why does the Pharisee say, "If he were a prophet"?
And again the most natural answer is: Because Jesus claimed
so to be.

Similarly several other traces, too often casually disregarded, point in the same direction. There is the often repeated word, now become a proverb, "a prophet is not without honor, save in his own country, and among his own kin,
and in his own house." [12] The word at the end of Jesus'
satirical reference to Herod Antipas, the local governor of

[9] Cf. the thoughtful essay by Hans Windisch, "Jesus und der Geist nach
synoptischer Überlieferung" in *Studies in Early Christianity*, edited by
Shirley Jackson Case, pp. 209–236.
[10] Luke 7:36–50.   [11] Mark 14:3–9; cf. Matt. 26:6–13.
[12] Mark 6:4; cf. Matt. 13:57; Luke 4:24; John 4:44.

Galilee, "... for it cannot be that a prophet perish out of Jerusalem,"[13] surely points in the same direction. In this connection, the word spoken by the two on the way to Emmaus, in answer to the then unknown stranger, "The things concerning Jesus the Nazarene, who was a prophet mighty in deed and word before God and all the people,"[14] evidences the ability of the later writer to allow his characters to speak in proper part.

As soon as this view of Jesus—a prophet sent from God— is recognized as the understanding of his first followers, who accepted wholeheartedly his own claim, many other elements in the gospel pages fall into place.

There is a constant reference to his possession of a spirit which has come upon him and possessed him. Opinions appear to have differed as to the origin of that spirit. To his followers it was palpably the spirit of God. To his opponents it was an evil spirit. But the point of significance is that there would seem no attempt by any one to deny that in the strictest and most literal sense of the word he was "inspired" by a spirit not his own.

To men of the first century this was a very easy and natural explanation of all activities outside the normal and the ordinary. Thus those whom today we would style insane were believed to be possessed by an evil spirit or spirits who had taken possession of them and were the source of their antics. The stories of exorcism—casting out of evil spirits—which are so common in the pages of the gospels, and which we shall have to consider in more detail later, make clear this view, as common in the first century as it is strange today. And in popular Jewish thinking the explanation of these evil spirits was ready to hand. They were the ghosts of the wicked

---

[13] Luke 13:33.   [14] Luke 24:19; cf. Matt. 21:11.

people who had perished in the flood. In the popular thinking, to paraphrase a line of the gospel song, "There are demons hovering 'round." And they were eager to take residence in men and women, thus once more to enjoy the bodily pleasures of life. This in essence would seem to explain the real motive in the ceremonial baths and washing, especially before eating and marriage. The basic purpose was, so to speak, to become spiritually antiseptic, to ward off the intrusion of evil demons, eager to enter the body and thus enjoy the satisfaction of food and the marriage bed.

On the contrary it was possible, especially in the past, to be similarly possessed by the Spirit of God. This was as great a blessing as possession by evil demons was a curse. This too was a view hallowed by age, and amply evidenced in the pages of the Old Testament. Superhuman strength, outstanding courage, great skill, unerring judgment, profound wisdom—all these are regularly attributed to the presence of the "Spirit of God" or "Spirit of the Lord," which comes upon a man and for the time being possesses him or, in more special cases, becomes his permanent endowment, even as in the case of Moses. The uninhibited stories of the prowess of Samson, whom the "Spirit of Yahweh began to move," [15] until his tragic loss of it through the wiles of Delilah, provide a sufficient example of this natural explanation of unusual prowess in the old narratives.

But in the developing thinking of Israel the Spirit of the Lord was specifically the Spirit of prophecy. It was the possession of Elijah and enabled him to be the mouthpiece of Yahweh and to perform his mighty deeds, both of kindness and of destruction. At the time of his translation it passed to Elisha, who had demonstrated his right to receive it. An especially clear picture of the prophet, convinced that

[15] Judg. 13:25.

he is the mouthpiece of God and that all who claim such
inspiration, but who differ from him, are possessed by lying
spirits sent to them by God for his own inscrutable purpose,
is to be found in the story of Micaiah, with his classic confidence: "As Yahweh liveth, what Yahweh saith unto me,
that will I speak." [16]

Possession of the Spirit of God and prophecy became fully
identified. In the thinking of what has come to be called
"normative Judaism" it had become a commonplace that
when Haggai, Zechariah, and Malachi—traditionally the last
of the prophets—died, the holy spirit departed from Israel.
All inspired men had been prophets, not alone those so
designated, but men like Abraham, Isaac, Jacob, Daniel,
Solomon, Ezra, and Mordecai. According to one old saying,
preserved in the Talmud,[17] there had been forty-eight
prophets and seven prophetesses who had prophesied to
Israel.

In the thinking of orthodox Judaism, at the time of the
ministry of Jesus, the age of revelation by prophetic agency
had ended when the Spirit was withdrawn. Whereas of old
God had declared his will through men especially chosen and
filled by him to be his mouthpiece, now his will was known
or knowable through the law, in which his complete and
entire revelation was to be found.

No serious study of the fascinating story of the development of Israel's classic contribution to world history, a literature passionately believed to be the direct and complete
revelation by God himself, can fail to see the influence of
the early prophets—Amos, Hosea, Micah, Isaiah, Jeremiah,
and Ezekiel—in its earlier stages. And it is equally clear that
as the view became dominant that their scriptures were this
complete revelation, the older medium of prophecy had

<hr/>

[16] I Kings 22:1–40.   [17] Megillah 14a.

gradually but effectively slipped into the background. The function of the prophet had lapsed. It was in the scripture that God's entire will and pleasure was to be discovered.

By the time of the Christian beginnings this view had become axiomatic. God, it was passionately believed, had revealed through the fathers and Moses a religion which was destined to become the universal religion of mankind. This revelation was entire and all-complete. Therein God had revealed his whole will and plan for mankind. Everything that men were to do, to think, to believe, to be, God had revealed to them. Moral conduct, the way they were to act toward one another and their creator—even their attitudes of mind and will—all this had been revealed and was man's for the knowing. Through the years it had been announced by God through the mouths and pens of worthies of the past, who had been in sober literalness merely the functioning organs of God. It was he, not they, who was thus the real author of Torah and of the subsequent and essentially equally authoritative Prophets and Writings.

Nor had this been a progressive revelation in the sense of change and development. Such concepts are unthinkable in a religion which takes itself seriously, as did Judaism, as one of revelation. From the very beginning, literally before the world was created, the whole blueprint was in the mind of God in its full and unalterable form. As the later rabbis phrased it: Among the seven things which were in the mind of God, created thus before he created the world, was the Law. For this commonplace Prov. 8:22 ff. was frequently cited as a proof text: "The Lord formed me as the first of his works, the beginning of his deeds of old." Thus everything which was ever to happen had been anticipated and recorded by God in this all-embracing act of revelation—his wondrous behest to his so dearly beloved and uniquely

endowed "chosen people." Some of the writings might be
late in coming; centuries had elapsed between Moses and
Isaiah, not to mention others far later than Isaiah. In all
of them, however, stood nothing which had not been in the
mind of God in the yesterdays before creation.

Thus of necessity there could be nothing really new. It had
all been anticipated. Things might *seem* new; they were not
so in actual fact. God never changes, never alters; whatever
now is under his blessing has always so been and could be
found in his all-inclusive revelation, had men but eyes to
see. This fundamental deduction, so central to all Jewish
thought, was to prove, it may be remarked in passing, of
great consequence in early Christian thinking as it viewed
itself in relation to God's purposes and destiny as the true
Judaism, and as it accordingly naturally found its own history, including the mission and death of its crucified Lord,
predicted and described throughout this all-inclusive revelation.

The basic conception that God had foreseen all the circumstances which would ever arise and had been at pains
to anticipate them, that all that was or ever would be at any
time under his blessing had always so been—*in posse* if not
in esse—finds expression again and again in views which
seem to the modern reader strange if not quixotic. To cite
but two examples: No good Jew could fail to celebrate the
Passover, nor could he imagine how it could ever have been
other. Thus we find the story that Abraham had been accustomed to celebrate it in his household. To be sure, its
origin was now believed to have been centuries later than
the patriarch, but God had communicated to this exemplary
figure what was destined to be. Or, the Law in all its completeness had been publicly communicated at Sinai in the
hearing of all mankind, for all those destined ever to be

born had been invisibly present at that awesome moment. Israel alone had accepted it, and hence had been blessed above all the rest of mankind. But through the years it had been in part forgotten and needed to be recovered, for, while it was all there, it was often implicit rather than explicit. The later so-called "unwritten law," that is, the oral tradition,[18] the accumulated learning of devoted and ingenious scholars, which in the century following Jesus began to be written down and which we know as the rabbinical literature—Mishnahs, Talmuds, and Midrashes—was simply the attempt to make explicit what they were convinced was implicit in the Law, God's greatest and most perfect gift to men.

Thus the scribes—interpreters of the word of God as written and custodians of the oral law, which sought to find in the written law the answers to the new problems constantly arising—had actually succeeded to or assumed the rôle earlier occupied by the prophets as God's spokesman. Yet, although God no longer commonly spoke through the prophets, on occasion he did speak by a mysterious voice (*bat kol*). Thus: "When the last prophets, Haggai, Zechariah, and Malachi, died, the holy spirit ceased out of Israel; but nevertheless it was granted to them to hear (*sc.* communications from God) by means of a mysterious voice." [19] Examples of this occasional "mysterious voice" may be seen in such stories as that of the ominous word to Nebuchadrezzar,[20] of the word at the baptism of Jesus,[21] at the transfiguration,[22] and at the time of climax,[23] heralded by the coming of the Greeks.

In addition, and of the most profound consequence, was

[18] Cf. Mark 7:1–23; Matt. 15:1–20.   [19] Tos. Sotah 13, 2.
[20] Dan. 4:31 f.   [21] Mark 1:11; Matt. 3:17; Luke 3:22.
[22] Mark 9:7; Matt. 17:5; Luke 9:35.   [23] John 12:28.

the confidence that in the future, once again, God would speak directly through the mouth of a prophet. The ancient word, attributed to none less than Moses himself, was explicit: "Yahweh thy God will raise up unto thee a prophet from the midst of thee."[24] In the speeches of Peter[25] and Stephen[26] this verse is quoted, and there can be but little question that it is seen fulfilled in Jesus. He had appeared as Moses had predicted he would.

That this is a postcrucifixion discovery appears to me improbable. Rather it is understood more naturally as a repetition of Jesus' own claim for himself. Once this assumption is made, many obscurities vanish. Nor does it appear to me at all impossible, or even improbable, that in this self-identification Jesus saw fulfilled the ominous word of Malachi, which a later generation of followers was to transfer to John the Baptist, whom they were viewing as the predecessor of Jesus: "Behold, I will send you Elijah the prophet before the great and terrible day of Yahweh come."[27]

What led the carpenter in Nazareth to the staggering conclusion that he had been chosen of God as his herald of the new age speedily to dawn, is impossible to explain. What led a Micaiah, an Amos, a Hosea, an Isaiah, a Saul of Tarsus, a Mohammed to essentially the same conclusion?

Modern attempts to minimize the significance of what may be easily styled the "prophetic complex," to make it understandable today and in line with the easy readiness of many clergymen—especially those who are less eager for the title priest—to consider themselves "prophets," are almost certain to obscure the ancient picture. The Semitic prophet was regarded, and regarded himself, as definitely

[24] Deut. 18:15.   [25] Acts 3:22.   [26] Acts 7:37.
[27] Mal. 4:5.

seized by the divine Spirit and subject to it. Thus the word
prophet was understood in the sense of *forth*teller, that is,
one speaking for another,[28] not a *fore*teller or simple pre-
dicter. Indeed the Hebrew word *nabi* has been considered
by some Semitists as the passive of the verb meaning "to
enter," and thus the "entered one." Whether this derivation
be etymologically correct or not, it emphasizes precisely the
Semitic view.

Thus the prophet never argues or teaches: he announces
the will of God which has been supernaturally revealed to
him. Opposition to his message is thus not opposition to him
but to the God who is speaking through him. A very clear
example of this confidence—be it styled conviction or mania
—is found in the word of Paul, which has often been regarded as a proof of that apostle's arrogance: "But though
we, or an angel from heaven, should preach unto you any
gospel other than that which we preached unto you, let him be
anathema. As we have said before, so say I now again, If
any man preacheth unto you any gospel other than that
which ye received, let him be anathema." [29]

But this is not conscious arrogance. Paul is convinced that
God had selected him, had endowed him with a divinely
inspired word. *Why* God had chosen him, he did not know;
that God had so done, he was unalterably convinced. Thus
when he spoke it was God who was speaking. Of course
what he said was true.

What was true of Paul was true of all the prophets, and
attempts to tone this down are folly. Attempts have frequently been made psychiatrically to explain this conviction
as an abnormal pathological obsession. Indeed Emil Ras-
mussen,[30] the Danish philologist, to cite but one, easily

---

[28] Cf. Exod. 7:1.   [29] Gal. 1:8 f.
[30] *Jesus: Eine vergleichende psychopathologische Studie.*

labeled all the prophets as epileptics. The diagnosis has
seemed to most students far too easy. That some of the
prophets, notably Ezekiel, not impossibly Paul, would be so
diagnosed today is very possible. Certain it is that in a literal
sense they saw visions, had mental experiences far from
what we call "normal." In the thought world of the ancient
east, accustomed as it was to such phenomena, this was far
less unnatural or an indication of mental perversity than at
the present day. Nor should it be overlooked that in men, as
in lamps, a wick turned too high, though it yields smoke, may
still give an intense light. Again it should not be forgotten
that rarely is this the only characteristic of the possessed
man. Along with the ability to be "snatched up into the third
heaven" and to "hear unspeakable words, which it is not
lawful for a man to utter,"[31] was often to be found the
staidest and most penetrating common sense.

That Jesus was in the same tradition is highly probable.
The prophet like unto Moses, long expected, had finally appeared. As the mouthpiece of God he uttered his call, confident that God through him was calling the nation to repentance and to ready itself for the final chapter. His passionate
confidence easily led to the conviction, seemingly shared by
his own family, that he was "beside himself"[32]—or, as we
would say, insane. To his opponents he was possessed by an
evil spirit.[33] To his followers these signs of "divine madness"
were patent proof that he was, as he himself apparently
believed, moved, possessed by the Spirit of God. To folk
accustomed to explain all the unusual, out-of-the-ordinary
experiences of life as due to the inworking of a supernatural
spirit, he may well have seemed an awesome and unusual
character. His scathing rebukes and impossible demands; his
amazing ability to exert a quieting and steadying influence

[31] II Cor. 12:2–5.   [32] Mark 3:21.   [33] Mark 3:22.

on others supernaturally distraught, and which may well have served as the solid historical basis for the many stories of his exorcising evil spirits; his understanding and sympathy for those on the outskirts of respectability; his ability with children; his unflinching, at times reckless, disregard of those in power; his amazing and absolute self-confidence which led him at times to seem to have all the answers and to utter them without qualifications or support—that such a many-faceted person, or personality, should have made the impress he so manifestly did, has never seemed to me passing strange. Our tendency—and a very mistaken one it has been —is to try to select some one of the facets and make it definitive, and then to be amazed that it should in his case have proved so revolutionary. If ever it has been true, it would seem to be true here, that the whole is vastly greater than the prosy arithmetical sum of its parts.

5

"The kingdom of God is at hand"

J ESUS' MESSAGE, as epitomized by Mark and substantially repeated by both Matthew and Luke—"The time is fulfilled, and the kingdom of God is at hand: repent ye, and believe this good news" [1]—is unmistakable in its meaning and has every appearance of being a strictly accurate report of his word.

The bell has sounded. The day so long expected by Israel has finally dawned. The sorry time of waiting is over. God's long-deferred promise is now to be realized. Convinced, as the prophet always is, that his word is not of his own imagination, but God's revelation which he need but sound, there can be but little question that Jesus started with confidence. Of course the people would hearken, and gladly. It was indeed "good news." God's greatest gift to man was speedily to be bestowed.

The tragedy of disillusion which the prophet so regularly faces is to discover that what is so certain to him, so crystal-

[1] Mark 1:15; cf. Matt. 4:17; Luke 4:15.

clear, is strangely obscure to others to whom it ought to be equally clear! In the case of Mohammed the only explanation that prophet could find was that Allah had strangely predestined many to close their ears to a truth so self-vindicating that otherwise none could have withstood. In Jesus the same bitter facts of life speedily became evident: the gate was strangely narrow, the way to life straitened. Many were refusing to enter in; but this could not affect the correctness of the word, God's word. It could only evidence that many hearts were sadly hardened against the truth.[2]

In the central phrase, "kingdom of God," there can be but little legitimate question as to what Jesus meant and what his hearers understood. This kingdom was the new age, the "Age to Come," which many apocalyptists had again and again in the past century expected and proclaimed. Attempts through the years to understand this phrase in terms of a gradual amelioration of society are far from impressive. Jesus' message was pitched in terms of the first century, not the twentieth. He was talking to Palestinian Jews, steeped in apocalyptic imagery and confident that when God saw the moment had come, he would act. The Age to Come, the new age, would suddenly and spectacularly appear. In soberest verity, despite its strangeness to modern ears, the end of the world was at hand.

Endless effort has been expended to soften and alter this unmistakable message, to make it conform to what men in each later age have been convinced was sound—and so, of course, the understanding of Jesus—and to the verdict of history. To the historian such attempts seem frivolous. When we let one who lived in the first century speak in that century, later attempts to modernize his thinking seem unnecessary, if not downright arrogant and presuming.

[2] Matt. 7:13–14; cf. Luke 13:23–24.

Great confusion, in no small part due to the desire to
modernize Jesus, has come from the endless debate as to
whether the kingdom he announced was present or future.
The confusion and debate seem unnecessary. The evidence
of the gospels and the unmistakable confidence of the early
followers of Jesus, so unambiguous and revealing in the
speeches in Acts and the letters of Paul, are that it is still
to come. As will be argued in more detail in a later chapter,
the kingdom would appear in the very immediate future,
but at the moment it was present only as are the clouds in
heaven which cast upon the earth their shadow. How one
can read the Greek gospels and Pauline letters and mistake
the undebatable "has drawn near," [3] is "near," [4] is hard to
fathom. The short and poignant petition in the Lord's prayer,
"Thy kingdom come," [5] should give pause to those who still
debate.

The picture is clear. The prophet of the speedy change
utters his warning. His countrymen are incessantly talking
about God, confident that they and they alone are his especially chosen, and deluding themselves with the unwarranted
confidence that they are obeying his commands. Let them
stop playing at life, turn to the Father, obey his commands,
recognize his sovereignty in the one way possible, namely,
by making their lives conform to it. In a word, let them start
living as they would in the kingdom were they fortunate
enough to gain the great boon: permission to enter.

Against this unambiguous and constant emphasis upon the
coming kingdom, which all students of the gospels have
frankly admitted must be so understood, are a comparatively
few passages which, it has been asserted, give a different

[3] ἤγγικεν (Mark 1:15; Matt. 3:2; 4:17; 10:7; Luke 10:9,11).
[4] ἐγγύς (Phil. 4:5).   [5] Matt. 6:10.

view, namely, of the gradual noncatastrophic growth of
something already present. The most frequently cited passage in this connection is the word, which Luke alone gives:
"The kingdom of God cometh not with observation: neither
shall they say, Lo, here! or, There! for lo, the kingdom of
God is *within* you." [6]

That this means an inward power, invisible and moving
men to gradual betterment, is thoroughly unlikely, as even
the succeeding verses of the context make plain. Actually,
while the pivotal words "within you" [7] may be so translated,
they are equally open to the rendering "in your midst." That
is, far from being in contrast, if not in flat contradiction, to
the other view, they are rather an even heightened stress
on the immediacy of the approach of a kingdom not yet
come. It is already within your grasp; you can, if you but
will, seize it. Its coming is so certain and in so immediate
a future that proleptically it may even be said: It is among
you, in your very midst.

Certainly it is proper criticism, when confronted by two
sorts of evidence—the one unmistakable in its meaning and
altered only by sheer violence; the other open to two interpretations, the one in conformity with the otherwise prevailing emphasis, the other possible only in sharp contrast
—to start with the certain and unmistakable and then to see
if without violence the other will conform; not to start with
the latter and the uncertain.

So here, the emphasis would seem to be: God's purpose
and intent are inevitable. He has spoken, and his will will
be fulfilled. Thus the Markan parable of the "Seed Growing
Secretly," [8] frequently cited in contrast to the dominant
view, is rather in complete accord. The seed has been sown.

[6] Luke 17:20 f.   [7] ἐντὸς ὑμῶν.   [8] Mark 4:26–29.

Nothing that man can do will thwart it. The harvest must
and will come. So also the even more familiar parables of the
Mustard Seed [9] and the Leaven.[10]

The kingdom comes of itself. It is in consequence of God's
initiative. It is not that Jesus brings it. Instead, God has
appointed him to announce its approach like Ezekiel's watchmen in the tower. To that extent it may be said that the
kingdom has brought Jesus. It comes of itself, unobserved,
impossible to detect by outward signs or clues, and quite
apart from man's efforts. In soberest reality it is the act of
God, not the deed of any man.

[9] Mark 4:30–32; Matt. 13:31–32; Luke 13:18–19.
[10] Matt. 13:33; Luke 13:20–21.

6

"Repent ye"

In mark's brief epitome of Jesus' word heralding the dawn of the new age, the advent of the kingdom,
stands also the pregnant word, Repent! Failure to obey God's
revealed will, heedless or deliberate violation—these had
spelled disaster. God's long-delayed promise of the dawn of
the glorious age, when all men everywhere would recognize
and obey his law, had been due to their flouting of his holy
will.

For Jesus, as for every pious Jew—unlike the Greeks
taught by such as Socrates—sin was not an error of judgment, an unwitting missing of the mark. Instead, it was
a deliberate and willful act of filial defiance to a gracious
and loving father. Thus in several of his parables Jesus gives
body and color to an insistent *Repent,* which in no Jewish
ear would seem strange. In the masterfully simple parable
of the two sons in the vineyard the note is crystal-clear.[1]
The father said, "Son, go work to-day in the vineyard." The
son replied, "I won't." In such a situation but one course of
action was possible. The son must repent of his folly, of his

[1] Matt. 21:28–32.

75

disobedience, must turn about and enter the vineyard. The
prodigal must turn about-face and return in rags from the
far country and implore the father's forgiveness.[2] The re-
pentant Zacchæus must restore fourfold.[3]

For centuries this insistence had seen central in Israel's
developing inheritance, stressed by every prophet: "Cease to
do evil; learn to do well."[4] And the point so often overlooked by casual readers of the New Testament, especially
of the Pauline letters, is that central in Jewish thinking—and
thoroughly shared by Jesus—was the confidence that man
could repent if he but would. Even before the creation of
the world, while yet God's all-inclusive Law was still in the
mind of God, coeval with it was the idea of repentance, for
God had realized that slips were bound to occur, that feet
would stumble: "He knoweth our frame; he remembereth
that we are dust."[5]

In a religion which took itself seriously as possessing a
complete revelation, or, to put it differently, which believed
that every practice of life had been ordained by God, sacrifice, which was an inheritance of the distant past, however
distasteful it might be to this prophet and that, was an
integral part. Of course it was to be performed. God had
ordained it. Interpreters of the law were not to narrow its
scope, were not to raise captious questions as to its efficacy
or why the lawgiver had so ordained it. He had, and that
was that. Yet—and the seemingly radical denial by some of
the prophets that God had ordained it may well have heightened this growing conviction—vain reliance upon sacrifice
was folly. Without being accompanied by a true and genuine
repentance it was useless. Thus the later rabbis saw in the

[2] Luke 15:11–32.   [3] Luke 19:1–10.   [4] Isa. 1:16 f.
[5] Psalm 103:14.

"fool's sacrifice" of Eccl. 5:1 [6] the act of those who sin and offer sacrifice but fail to secure their forgiveness because they have failed to repent.[7] Without a genuine repentance and all that it involves, no rite is efficacious.

The origin of the ceremony of the scapegoat may well be obscure. As practised by later Judaism it too makes very clear the central place that repentance had come to play. The sanctuary might still be anointed with blood. The animal was still driven forth. But that the desired effect was not obtained by the physical disinfection of the temple or even by the physical bearing away of the sins—efficacious as these acts may once have been believed to be—is clear from the confession of the people, said over the animal by the high priest:

O God, thy people, the House of Israel, have committed iniquity, transgressed, and sinned before thee. O God, forgive, I pray, the iniquities and transgressions and sins which thy people, the house of Israel, have committed and transgressed and sinned before thee; as it is written in the law of thy servant, Moses, *For on this day shall atonement be made for you to cleanse you: from all your sins shall ye be clean before the Lord.*[8]

The desired restitution, reconciliation, atonement was achieved, not by the efficacy of the rites, but solely by the forgiveness of God.

Here is to be seen why, as the years went by, the mechanics of sacrifice declined in actual importance in the life of Israel. By the ancient Deuteronomic reform, which had limited sacrifice to Jerusalem, only a tiny percentage of Jews

[6] "Keep thy foot when thou goest to the house of God; for to draw nigh to hear is better than to give the sacrifices of fools, for they know nothing but to do wrong."

[7] Cf. Berakot 23a.

[8] Mishnah Yoma 6, 2. This prayer is ascribed to R. Judah (*ca.* A.D. 150).

could ever have any actual part in it. And more and more in the representative thinking of the nation the temple—preserver of the ancient customs, still jealously guarded by the priests and their devotees, flocked to by pilgrims—ceased to be the real centre of Jewish life. It remained a glamorous symbol, a visual proof of the nearness of Yahweh. To it thousands of pilgrims surged on each feast day, anxious to assemble, at least once in their lifetime, to "Zion whither the tribes go up." But the uncompromising ethical demands, the insistence that without a deep and genuine repentance a man's sacrifice was worse than useless—this had sounded the death knell of the temple as the actual centre of Jewish life.

All this is seen very clear in the fact that Judaism took in its stride the fall of the temple in A.D. 70, and the complete cessation of sacrificial expiation which this of necessity involved. The loss was keenly felt, and wrath at the destroyers was bitter. But the real temper of Judaism is well revealed in the story of the conversation between the famed rabbi Johanan ben Zakkai, and his disciple, Joshua ben Hananiah. As they passed the temple in ruins, the younger man exclaimed in sorrow: "Woe to us, for the place where the iniquities of Israel were atoned for is destroyed!" The master replied: "Do not grieve, my son, for we have an atonement which is just as good, namely, deeds of mercy, as the Scripture says, *For I desire mercy and not sacrifice.*" The story is late,[9] but the insight is not. From the days of Amos and Hosea that note had been sounded, and not without avail. Jeremiah had given it his unforgettable support. Again and again the same refrain had been sounded in the Psalms.

It is against this background and this context that Jesus' imperious demand, "Repent," is to be seen. It is a demand for change of conduct as well as of heart. Everything incompat-

[9] Abot de R. Nathan 4, 5.

ible with the new kingdom must be laid aside. As the mer-
chantman gladly sells all his other possessions to acquire the
priceless pearl,[10] or as the man who upon discovery of a
hidden treasure does not rest until he has acquired it,[11] so
the wise man will consider nothing of consequence save being found worthy of entering the new age so speedily to
dawn. Neither comfort nor even physical well being is to
be compared with the one priceless boon. What is an eye
or a hand or a foot—parts of a perishable body—in comparison with this? Should they be a hindrance, a lure to sin
and so of exclusion, their loss is an inestimable boon.[12] These
and other demands, which have often been toned down or
dismissed as "oriental hyperbole," become entirely intelligi-
ble when one who lived in the first century is allowed to
act and speak as such.

Thus few things would seem more certain than that Jesus
believed passionately in the near approach of the universal
sovereignty of God which, as he viewed it, was the apocalyptic "age to come." This was the good news which he so
insistently proclaimed.

---

[10] Matt. 13:45–46.   [11] Matt. 13:44.
[12] Mark 9:43–48; Matt. 18:8–9; cf. Matt. 5:29–30.

7

"And believe this good news"

THIS MESSAGE which Jesus proclaimed was indeed "good news." It is this difference in tone which is the real difference between Jesus and the earlier prophets, or, to speak more exactly, which differentiated the earlier "prophecy" from the later "apocalyptic." Josephus is correct in his stressing the difference between the older prophets and Daniel, although, of course, he errs in his view that Daniel was written in the days of the Exile:

> ... And while the prophets used to foretell misfortunes, and on that account were disagreeable both to the kings and to the multitude, Daniel was to them a prophet of good things, and this to such a degree that, by the agreeable nature of his predictions, he procured the good will of all men.[1]

During the days when the kingdom still stood, even though the clouds were thickening and disaster inevitable, the prophets, from Amos to Ezekiel, had only words of unqualified doom. When Jerusalem, despite its temple, fell and the prophecies of disaster were seen to be true, not only did

[1] Josephus, *Antt.* 10, 11, 7.

it give stature to the "disagreeable" harbingers of woe and reveal them as "true prophets," in contradistinction to those now easily seen to be "false," [2] but, of necessity it tended to raise new problems.

From the time of the Exile, no longer was the word of unqualified doom in point. The blow had fallen. The nation was humbled. The thing long feared had come. Gradually from now on the element of hope for the future for the now chastened and humbled nation begins to make its appearance. And regularly, as the years went by, the words of the older prophets—still in a fluid and "uncanonized" form— were edited with happy endings and rays of hope, which seemed as natural to the generation which produced them as they are incongruous and out of place in our more historically accurate survey.

During the two centuries of Persian control the type of thinking which we today style "apocalyptic" had made its impress. While much of its lush imagery and catastrophic insistence was never wholeheartedly adopted by the leaders and professional teachers of later Judaism,[3] it was increasingly popular among the common people, and through that channel came to be highly acceptable in the eyes of early Christians.

Its insistence upon the speedy collapse of the present age —to those poor and oppressed, the "present *evil* age"—and the dawn of a new and very different age was naturally most attractive in the eyes of those who had nothing to lose and everything to gain by such a change. And it was easy to see this change in terms of a restored Israel victorious over its heathen and wicked oppressors. Thus during the days of the Syrian oppression, which led to the Maccabean rebel-

---

[2] Deut. 18:20–22; cf. 13:1 ff.
[3] It is conspicuously absent from both Midrashim and Talmuds.

lion, and latterly under the absolute control of Rome, it is
small wonder that this incendiary literature of crisis should
have become increasingly popular.

It is probably not too rash to suggest that for each of the
authors of this "newer prophecy"—of which the canonical
Daniel is our best early example, and the book of Revelation
a fair sample of the later years—there had been some especial crisis which proved to him that the end was at hand. In
this type of thinking the one thing certain was that the
change would be wrought by God himself, who would
mightily intervene. In a word, the instant before sunrise is
always the darkest moment; or reversed, this darkest moment
presages the dawn.

Thus to the author of Daniel it was the hellish acts of
Antiochus Epiphanes which *proved* that the end was at
hand. Nothing more hideous could be conceived. Thus God
must intervene. Similarly it is more than probable that two
centuries later—shortly after the crucifixion of Jesus—it was
the insane determination of the Roman emperor Gaius
(Caligula) to set up his statue in the holy of holies of the
Jerusalem temple which sparked another similar apocalypse,
portions of which are preserved in somewhat altered form in
the Synoptic gospels and placed in the mouth of Jesus.[4]

The precise act which so infuriated one particular author
may not have seemed especially or uniquely significant to
others. For example, there can be but little question that it
was the outrage of "emperor worship" which prompted the
blasting anti-Roman tract, our Book of Revelation, sparked
very possibly by some especial act or incident. But con-
temporaneously the author of I Peter, while no Quisling, was
insisting, as had Paul before him[5]: "Fear God. Honor the
king,"[6] that is, the Roman emperor.

---

[4] Mark 13:5–37; Matt. 24:4–36; Luke 21:8–36.   [5] Rom. 13:1–7.
[6] I Pet. 2:17.

It is possible to dismiss these later "prophets" as alarmists, who in the perfervid excitement which some abhorrent incident or event aroused, were sure that *this* was the certain prelude to the long-expected end. Such name-calling should not blind the student to the fact that though their prediction of the end failed—as have those of their many equally certain successors—for all of them the future was rosy, not black. Unlike the earlier prophets of doom, they were harbingers of hope: "a few more marchings weary, then we'll gather home." Thus their words were words of "good news," which they were certain would be eagerly accepted and believed.

In this respect Jesus of Nazareth seems to have been one of this number, although unlike many of those known to us he wrote no book. Instead, like the earlier prophets of doom, he was a "speaking," not a "writing," prophet. Unlike them his word was one of convinced, joyful hope, not of despair.[7]

Once again we can ponder the question, already several times suggested: What started Jesus? What convinced him that the Day was about to dawn, that the time of waiting was over, that God himself was about to intervene? At our remove, any definite answer is, of course, but a guess. That it had resulted from the activity of John the Baptist would seem, as already mentioned, most unlikely. That some definite event led him to the conviction that he must speak *now* would seem to me rather more probable than that it was simply the result of long reflection or "deepening of conviction."

---

[7] It is quite possible that the technical term, as we now view it, "gospel" ($\epsilon\dot{\upsilon}\alpha\gamma\gamma\acute{\epsilon}\lambda\iota o\nu$), which means literally "good news," arose and became a technical name for the resulting Christian credo, and still later for the books which contained it, in natural consequence of the fact that it echoed precisely the word which Jesus had used to characterize his herald's word from God.

During Pilate's ten years as procurator (governor) of the Province of Judea, several incidents leading to indignant outbursts are known to us [8]—the carrying into Jerusalem of the imperial standards, the use of temple money for the building of an aqueduct, the matter of the votive shields— and there may have been others which seemed to this individual or that of especial heinousness. Nor should we forget the incident casually referred to in Luke 13:1, "Now there were some present at that very season who told him (i.e., Jesus) of the Galileans, whose blood Pilate had mingled with their sacrifices." Any of these might conceivably have provided the spark for Jesus. But none of this is certain, perhaps even probable. It may well have been some more local, Galilean incident, of which Herod Antipas, the governor of that territory, provided no small few.[9]

What it was we shall never know. But like Amos before him, to whom the roar of the lion, heard in the solitary darkness as he guarded his flocks,[10] may well have been the spark that kindled his tinder, it is far from improbable that *something* had occurred which led the carpenter in Nazareth to believe that at long last the day was about to dawn and— even more soul-shattering—that God had appointed him to stand before the nation and to herald this good, if startling, news.

[8] See pp. 202–204.

[9] Actually, the murder of John the Baptist is not to be forgotten as the possible spark, even though Jesus had not been personally involved in John's movement or numbered among his disciples.

[10] Amos 3:4.

8

"The time is fulfilled"

THAT THIS catastrophic change—the appear-
ance of the kingdom, the dawn of the new age, the end of
the world—would take place immediately, at any instant,
would seem to be the certain conviction of the new prophet.
Despite the repeated and insistent attempts to deny this or
to tone it down, to make it conform to the subsequent very
different verdict of history, it must be asserted without
qualification that its denial leaves the gospel story and the
activity of the first two generations of followers of the crucified prophet bristling with question marks.

For the early followers of the crucified Jesus the one great
certainty was the immediate dawn of the new age. The movement was primarily a missionary movement, to spread that
word and to make men ready.

No heedful reading of the Pauline letters can fail to see
this as Paul's certain belief. The fullest and most explicit
statement stands in his first letter to Thessalonica. It was
prompted by the sorrow and confusion that had arisen in
that newly founded group because some of their number

had died in the short interval between Paul's visit to them
and the time of writing. In reply Paul wrote explicitly:

But we would not have you ignorant, brethren, concerning
them that fall asleep; that ye sorrow not, even as the rest, who
have no hope. For if we believe that Jesus died and rose again,
even so them also that are fallen asleep in Jesus will God bring
with him. For this we say unto you by the word of the Lord, that
we that are alive, that are left unto the coming of the Lord, shall
in no wise precede them that are fallen asleep. For the Lord
himself shall descend from heaven, with a shout, with the voice
of the archangel, and with the trump of God: and the dead in
Christ shall rise first; then we that are alive, that are left, shall
together with them be caught up in the clouds, to meet the Lord
in the air: and so shall we ever be with the Lord. Wherefore
comfort one another with these words.[1]

To attempt to deny that Paul was convinced—and had
convinced his converts—that this spectacular event would
occur in the immediate future, surely in their lifetime, is
idle. It may very well be that in the common-sense ethical
advice of this doughty man were timeless emphases; nonetheless they were in very fact interim ethics. It is of importance to remember that what is patent in Paul is no less
likely for Jesus. The holding of views which to a later age
may seem quixotic (and, in the light of the verdict of history, incorrect) need by no means prevent a man from also
holding and expressing the soundest God-given common
sense. In a word, Paul might—and surely did—believe the
world was going to end on the morrow. On the other hand,
he labored and taught as if it would last forever. At times,
what may seem at first glance a most surprising inconsistency
is seen to be, when viewed on a larger canvas, of great
moment.

This word of Paul to the Thessalonians is far from being

[1] I Thes. 4:13–18.

the only indication of his confidence that the end was at hand. "Behold, I tell you a mystery: We all shall not sleep, but we shall all be changed, in a moment, in the twinkling of an eye, at the last trump: for the trumpet shall sound, and the dead shall be raised incorruptible, and we shall be changed." [2] "And this, knowing the season, that already it is time for you to awake out of sleep: for now is salvation nearer to us than when we first believed. The night is far spent, and the day is at hand. . . ." [3]

In the light of words like these it is impossible to deny that when Paul said, The "Lord is at hand," [4] he meant it literally. Nor is this view to be seen as a uniquely Pauline view. On the contrary, this expectation was the mainspring of the early movement, the confidence which lent strength to their legs and fire to their words. To regard it as a later and curious aberration which somehow arose and came to be read back is to misunderstand completely the early movement. Actually, it was as the decades passed and the expected event did not arrive that the problem arose and the earlier confidence seemed fronted with the direst consequences.

In our gospels are words which it is absurd to view as produced by a later day and read back. Conspicuous among them is the word, "Verily, I say unto you, There are some here of them that stand by, who shall in no wise taste of death, till they see the kingdom of God come with power." [5] Matthew's repetition of this word prevents a modern "un-Markan" toning down of the word, "coming of the kingdom," for Matthew is explicit: "There are some of them that stand here, who shall in no wise taste of death, till they see the Son of man coming in his kingdom." [6]

To regard a word such as this as having been produced—

[2] I Cor. 15:51–52.   [3] Rom. 13:11–12.   [4] Phil. 4:5.
[5] Mark 9:1.   [6] Matt. 16:28.

invented, and put in the mouth of Jesus—at a time when
his generation *had* passed and when it was thus palpably
and grotesquely impossible of fulfillment surely needs no
refutation. As has been sententiously remarked: "One does
not use battering-rams on gates that stand open."

That such a word might be preserved and explained or
interpreted in what seemed the light of later experience is
one thing. We have hosts of such examples, embalmed and
rendered innocuous by "later insights." That it should have
been produced *de novo* when its fulfillment was demon-
stratedly impossible is quite another. Nor can the historian
be satisfied with the explanation of those who feel the force
of this argument but attempt to free Jesus from the responsibility of sharing—better said, initiating—the belief which
was destined never to be fulfilled, by arguing that its origin
was very early, at a time when it could (in theory) be fulfilled, but was not his but the view of his first followers who
misunderstood his meaning.

Superficially this may seem for the moment attractive and
to free Jesus from views which we see now to have been
mistaken and which, in view of what we think we know of
the universe in which we live, if held and proclaimed today,
would indicate a mental unbalance of very marked degree.
But the attractiveness of this "saving hypothesis"—which
after all is quite unnecessary since Jesus lived in first-century
Palestine, not in twentieth-century America—is but superficial. It leaves one with but two alternative conclusions, and
neither of them is attractive or necessary. Either Jesus was
so singularly inept a teacher that he could not make clear to
his hearers the message nearest to his heart and which was,
as he passionately believed, inspired by God; or else his
chosen followers were obtuse to such a sorry degree as to
make it scarcely reasonable to suppose that if they failed to

understand here, their understanding was any better at other points, and that therefore we have no just ground for assuming the reliability of any part of the record.

And this is but heightened when one realizes, as the evidence seems to demand, that Jesus made so tremendous an impression upon some—in my judgment, many—of his hearers that even his death could not shake their confidence that he had been "the prophet sent by God." That with their confidence (which, as will be later argued, led to the conviction that he had triumphed, i.e., had been, as later followers came to phrase it, "raised from the dead") they were either careless of his word or ready to revise it or substitute another for it, is far more difficult to understand than the alleged difficulty it so awkwardly seeks to explain away.

Neither of the two hypotheses appears attractive or necessary. They are but a part of the critically vicious notion that none save Jesus himself—and, of course, a few twentieth-century Americans, horrified at the contention that Jesus did not share their views—knew what he meant. My impression is that there was nothing obscure at all so far as his message was concerned. His hearers knew perfectly well what he meant. It became the missionary gospel of those who found it attractive; it was the cause of his death at the hands of his enemies, who crucified him, not because they did not understand it, but rather because they did.

9

"And the common people heard him gladly"

THAT AT THE TIME of his death Jesus was forsaken by all and died alone, save for a few women who viewed the tragedy from afar, is the common picture. During the last weeks of his ministry he had limited himself to the small group of twelve disciples, in no small part due to the fact that there had been a great dropping off of those who had earlier listened to his words. And of the Twelve, one had betrayed him, another had denied him, all had fled the city in terror. Speedily, however, this had changed. Within a few short weeks the Twelve were once more in Jerusalem and making converts at a prodigious rate, three thousand in a single day.[1]

This popular picture has appealed greatly to many readers of the gospel story. The contrast between the unrelieved gloom of the Good Friday evening and the sudden dawn of the Easter morning has seemed to many to be explainable

[1] Acts 2:41.

90

solely by the congenial mystic word: "God did it." By the miracle of the Resurrection, and by it alone, was the amazing rightabout-face made possible.

And this explanation has been highly acceptable to many theologians as well. It assures them of the centrality of the Resurrection, seems to warrant the confidence still so insistently held that this, and this alone, was the sole "kerygma," the message, of the now transformed disciples.

The peril of this popular explanation is that it opens wide the doors to a tacit neglect of all that preceded Calvary. Had not God performed a stupendous miracle on the body of the crucified Jesus, the latter's work had failed. It was that which was done to his body which had convinced his followers. What he had been to them would otherwise have been of no consequence.

To me, this oft-repeated view smacks too much of the device—*deus ex machina*—employed by some of the early Greek dramatists to rescue their plots from the intricacies which they had skillfully depicted but could not resolve. And it is so completely unnecessary. Had not his companions become convinced—perhaps more deeply than some of them at the moment realized—of the rightness of his claim to be a prophet sent by God, it is highly improbable that they would have seen him on the Easter morning. It was the deathless confidence he had roused in his hearers that by the power of God he had spoken as "no other man spake" which led to their passionate belief that he must have triumphed over death and was still alive. The later conventional stories of the Resurrection—supernatural appearances, resuscitated body, empty tomb—were the inevitable *result* of this all-central confidence, not its *cause*. To fail to see this is to strip Jesus of his true significance and to make of him but one more puppet in an otherworldly drama. The cost of this blindness has been heavy. The real Jesus has vanished, to be replaced by the Christ of faith.

Nor is it hard to discover the source of this confusion—this viewing the result as the cause. It is, once again, the basic misstatement so constantly repeated: no one knew who he was. And the real source of this costly error is to be found in the book which has so deeply influenced all subsequent thinking, the Gospel of Mark.

Too long this book has been casually dismissed as a partial collection of incidents remembered and artlessly put together by one who had listened to—and perhaps translated—the preaching of Peter. In contrast to the Gospel of John, which has long been recognized as entirely theological, stands the Gospel of Mark, which at the end of the last century had come to be regarded as entirely historical. The ditch between the two, we are now coming to see, has been dug too wide and deep. It is not that the Gospel of John is "more like the Synoptists," notably Mark, than reckless critics had allowed at the end of the battle waged by D. F. Strauss, F. C. Baur, and H. J. Holtzmann against the priority of John. Rather we have come to see that the Synoptists—and again, notably, the Gospel of Mark—are far more like John than we had realized.

And this likeness consists in Mark's definite theological concern. The author is concerned with but one basic problem: the hostility which Jesus aroused and which had ended in his crucifixion. Why, if Jesus was what Mark was certain that he was, namely, the one sent by God and anointed by him for the service he was to render, which culminated in his death whereby he gave his life as a ransom for many— why was he crucified? Why was he misunderstood so tragically by all, including even his own disciples who fled in terror? And Mark's answer was: they did not know. It was only later, in the light of the Resurrection, that they knew.

Mark's account thus opens with the dramatic word: "The time is fulfilled." The two preceding incidents—baptism and temptation—are part of his prologue. Jesus had appeared, had been endued by the Spirit, had been driven by its compulsion into the wilderness, where, like Elijah before him, he had been miraculously fed by the angels, and had successfully met and worsted the demons (the "wild beasts"), and thereby knew with certainty that the end was at hand, that the cosmic bell had sounded.

None but Jesus—and the demons!—know who he is. They know and tremble at every subsequent meeting. Even his disciples do not know, although as the days pass they gain a partial, but woefully limited, dawning insight. They are destined to know, and Jesus, without ever making any claims or direct statements, allows them to see what he does and hear what he says. To the others, destined not to understand, he talks in parables in order that they may not understand.[2] To the disciples he privately explains the parables.

The story moves to its turning point. They are crossing the lake.[3] The disciples are worried because they have but one loaf in the boat. Jesus rebukes them. Have they not seen the repeated miracle of the feeding of the Five and of the Four Thousand? Do they not yet understand? Shortly after they prove that they do—in part![4] In answer to the question: "Who say ye that I am?" Peter makes his proper reply, "Thou art the Christ." Jesus, after first warning Peter not to herald

---

[2] Mark 4:10–12. It is patent that this "purpose," which has so regularly shocked readers, is a later and purely artificial explanation and in no wise reflects Jesus' own reason for using these illuminating illustrations. Similarly, the labored explanations of their meaning (cf. Mark 4:13–20), purportedly told to the Twelve privately, are certainly later additions, not part of the original parable, nor to be ascribed to Jesus himself.

[3] Mark 8:14–21.   [4] Mark 8:27–33.

this abroad, now begins to tell them the tragic secret: his coming death and resurrection. At once Peter, again the spokesman, protests and receives a rebuke. Twice more Jesus announces to them, and to them only, his coming death and immediate triumph "after three days"; [5] but to the end they cannot see it, and when it happens, precisely as foretold to them, they are strangely unready, strangely unwilling to await the outcome of the "three days"!

When this Markan account is viewed as sober history, many unanswerable problems arise, some of which may for the moment be reserved. But there are two other all-important elements in the Markan picture to be considered. Directly following Peter's confession occurs the Transfiguration, with another word from God, strangely reminiscent of the earlier word at the baptism.[6] The former had told Jesus— and, artistically, the reader of the Markan narrative!—who he was. The word at the Transfiguration is the necessary conclusion to Peter's confession: "This is my beloved Son: hear ye him." That is, Peter was right in his dawning recognition; pitifully wrong in his refusal to believe the word that Jesus "must suffer many things, and be rejected by the elders, and the chief priests, and the scribes, and be killed, and after three days rise again." *That* was the word he was to "hear," that is, to accept and believe. And neither Peter nor his fellow disciples learned the lesson—until after the Resurrection.

The other incident makes the matter certain. Following the fateful crossing of the lake and Jesus' haunting question: "Do ye not yet understand?" they had met a blind man.[7] In answer to the plea to heal him, Jesus had put spit in his eyes and placed his hands upon him. The cure was but partial:

[5] Mark 9:30–32; 10:32–34. [6] Mark 9:2–8.
[7] Mark 8:22–26.

he saw men moving about, but they looked like trees. Once more the laying on of hands, and he saw clearly.

This little incident, bristling with difficulties if it is to be regarded as an actual event (and omitted by both Matthew and Luke, almost certainly because, in their eyes, it was a far from satisfactory sort of cure by one who, even at a distance, could speak and cause the perfect cure to occur at once), is far from incidental to Mark. It is all-important, the paradigm of the disciples themselves. The partial sight of the blind man is the partial sight of the disciples: "Thou art the Christ." But it is only partial because of their tragic inability to accept the all-necessary consequences. They reached the second stage, seeing "all things clearly," only in the light of the Resurrection.

In this connection the word of Paul, which is basic to his outlook, is of significance: Jesus, who was prophesied in the Scriptures and was born of the seed of David, "was declared to be the Son of God with power . . . *from his resurrection from the dead*." [8] He was God's son before his death; it was only in the light of the Resurrection that he effectively and convincingly was seen so to be. To what extent Mark knew and was influenced by Paul's thinking is uncertain and need not concern us now. What is certain is that Mark has extended the "shadow of the cross" back into the life of Jesus. To Peter the divine annunciation came in consequence of his partial insight; to Jesus—and to the reader of the gospel!—it had been given at the very start of the ministry.

The consequences of this "theological explanation" of the otherwise baffling enigma: "Why, if he was what he was, did men treat him as they did?" have been tremendous. This gospel set the patterns for all subsequent thinking. And when it came to be regarded as "baldly historical," it seemed to

[8] Rom. 1:1–5.

justify the notion—so eagerly, if mistakenly, adopted—that no one knew or comprehended his word.

In this connection, the Markan theory that after this "dawning insight" Jesus limited himself severely to those who were destined to know, that is, to the Twelve, led not unnaturally to the notion that since they and they alone were his audience, the earlier crowds which had hung on his words had lost their earlier interest. Mark does not so say, and many indications to the contrary are present in his developing narrative,[9] but the consequent impression is not surprising. This is heightened by a word in the Gospel of John. Although most critics are today very cautious in their use of the Gospel of John for historical details, this particular word continues to be utilized despite its patently artificial context.

The story of the feeding of the Five Thousand is retold in this gospel and transformed into the account of the establishment of the Eucharist. In the subsequent account of the Last Supper, all reference to the bread and wine has vanished. It was in the discourse following the earlier Feeding of the Five Thousand that the theme of "eating my flesh and drinking my blood" was developed. "Upon this many of his disciples went back, and walked no more with him."[10] It can scarcely be doubted that this statement was influential in establishing the notion of a falling away of the crowds. Even after this gospel itself had lost its earlier standing as an historic source, this view of the ministry persisted, for it was seemingly the explicit expression of what seemed the Markan contention. And this Johannine word (6:66) was the prelude to the Johannine equivalent of Peter's confession.[11]

In contrast to the picture of a dwindling audience and a

[9] Notably Mark 10:32–34.   [10] John 6:66.
[11] Cf. John 6:66–71 with Mark 8:27–33. It was Judas, not Peter, who had been labeled "Satan," that is, "a devil."

complete obtuseness to the real meaning of Jesus' imperious word, which could be rectified only by the supernatural intervention of God, it is the contention of this book that all this is quite unlikely; that instead, the word of Mark already employed as the title of this chapter, "And the common people heard him gladly," is solidly historical, and that there is no slightest reason to postulate any cooling of enthusiasm on the part of his hearers, still less of any uncertainty as to the meaning of his words.

10

"Blessed are ye poor"

ALONG WITH the revealing and seemingly historically sound word, "And the common people heard him gladly," there are constant repetitions to this effect in the gospel stories. Jesus is contemptuously styled by his opponents "a friend of publicans and sinners," [1] i.e., of the riffraff. In this connection the word "Judge not, that ye be not judged" [2] assumes an importance often overlooked. During the centuries of approbation of this attractive sentiment, one which has aided in forming the romantic picture of the tenderhearted and almost effeminately "gentle Jesus," it is regularly overlooked that there were many in Israel toward whom his attitude was seemingly far from "Judge not." Instead, his words with regard to the leaders and the well-to-do were bitterly critical and censorious, if correctly reported, not alone in Matthew's frequent expansions, but in the briefer more restrained accounts in Mark. There is little indication that in his eyes the scribes and Pharisees were to be included in the demand for absence of judging.

Nor is the reason for this exception hard to see. Through

[1] Matt. 11:19; Luke 7:34. [2] Matt. 7:1.

the years commentators and preachers have sought labori-
ously, and a bit self-consciously, to explain away what might
seem an inconsistency. When cogent argument failed, the
answer was always easy: He was not as other men, and
ordinary human standards of consistency are out of place.
With a reasonable and natural explanation ready to hand,
such explanations would appear quite unnecessary.

Again, it has been not infrequently commented that there
is in the gospels a marked opposition, even hostility, to
wealth. But once more, the seemingly obvious explanation
has been lost sight of. "Blessed are ye poor: for yours is the
kingdom of God. Blessed are ye that hunger now: for ye shall
be filled" [3]: these beatitudes, especially in conjunction with
the parallel woes ("Woe unto you that are rich! for ye have
received your consolation." "Woe unto you, ye that are full
now! for ye shall hunger" [4]), are clear-cut and unqualified.
It would hardly seem necessary to argue that they are distinctly earlier and more original than the Matthœan version:
"Blessed are the poor in spirit" and "Blessed are they that
hunger and thirst after righteousness." [5] These latter have
a grace and charm which assure them a lasting place in our
tradition, quite despite their obvious secondary quality.

The same primitive note is struck very clearly in the story
of the Rich Man (Dives) and Lazarus.[6] If we are content
to read the story as it stands and without gratuitous additions, its emphasis is unmistakable. Here are two men, the
one very rich, the other miserably poor. There is no slightest
hint that the one is bad, the other good. They die. One goes
to a hell of torment, the other to blessed joy. And the reason
is clear: the one was rich, the other poor. This has occasionally been lost sight of, due to another detail in the story

[3] Luke 6:20–21.   [4] Luke 6:24–25.   [5] Matt. 5:3, 6.
[6] Luke 16:19–31.

—the dogs who "came and licked his sores." This detail has been absurdly seen as a contrast to the indifference of the hardhearted rich man: the devoted little puppy nuzzling the poor and lonely outcast. This may seem an attractive interpretation to modern Americans with a fondness for pet dogs. In the mid-East—then or now—no such notion would ever be read in and out. Here was but one more evidence of Lazarus' wretchedness. Even the pariah dogs, so common and offensive in every village, added to his misery by slobbering over his sores.

In a word, this perfectly natural story is in entire accord with the Magnificat [7] and the coming reversal: those in high places shall be brought low, those of low degree shall be raised on high; the hungry shall be filled with good things, the rich sent empty away. That this exquisite lyric was the spontaneous outburst of the little Palestinian maid, Mary, is surely open to more than serious doubt. It explains in chaste and lovely phrase a basic emphasis in what may be safely called the lowest, that is, the earliest, stratum of the gospel story.

A third example is to be found in the classic story of the rich man and Jesus, commonly styled the Rich Young Ruler, in consequence of Matthew's retouching of the Markan story.[8] Here again the emphasis is inescapable: the man has accepted Jesus' word and wishes to "have eternal life," that is, to enter the kingdom which he has been told and believes is speedily to dawn. Despite his exemplary life there is one insuperable obstacle: "One thing thou lackest." He has wealth, and a rich man cannot enter the kingdom. As a pious Jew, Jesus will not declare anything impossible for God; what he does say is that only by an unlikely miracle of God

---

[7] Luke 1:46-55.   [8] Mark 10:17-31; Matt. 19:16-30; Luke 18:18-30.

could it happen. The vivid imagery of the camel and the eye of the needle is not to be blunted by the occasional insipid attempts to avoid a clear but unacceptable insistence. Thus endeavors to see in the phrase "needle's eye" a reference to a narrow street, popularly (and imaginatively) styled "fat man's misery," or to dally with learned-sounding nonsense that in place of "camel" (κάμηλον) a similar-sounding Greek word, "cable" (κάμιλον), is to be substituted are simply absurd.[9] Wealth is an insuperable bar to entrance into the kingdom.

All attempts—and they have been many—to tone this down actually highlight the original insistence. There is no slightest evidence that this was a special diagnosis of a special man; that in his case, Jesus saw with penetrating eye that *his* wealth was to him a handicap. Certainly the shocked word of Jesus' disciples, "Who then can be saved?" and Jesus' unqualified retort that only by a literal miracle of God can such a hindrance be removed are perfectly clear. Nor, it may be remarked in passing, is there the slightest hint that Jesus' concern is to have the property distributed to aid the underprivileged. As we shall subsequently see, this not uncommon deduction is quite unwarranted. Jesus is not concerned here with relieving the needs of the poor—that will be done by God in the immediate future when the kingdom

[9] In addition to the reasonable certainty that the original reading is *camel*, not *cable*, it must be remarked that to thread a hawser through the eye of a needle is no essential easing of a hard figure. It would still be a miracle. This raises an important point often overlooked: to some there may seem to be a gradation in the "size" of miracles and a consequent tendency to "heighten the miraculous" by superficial alteration. Most people would find it as difficult to change one teaspoonful of water into wine as 150 gallons. By multiplying the figures one does not pass from an "easy" to a "hard" miracle. Thus we may with confidence leave "camel" in the text. And camels were as commonly seen in Palestine as they are rare in America or Western Europe.

dawns. Jesus is concerned with this man himself. Unless he rids himself of his dreadful fetter, the door for him will be barred.

This distrust of wealth, so evident in the earliest stratum of the gospel record, although gradually lessened, as we shall see, as the years passed, very probably accurately reflects the attitude of Jesus himself. But, to use a bit of modern technical jargon, it may well have been "an acquired characteristic," a consequence of his own experience, rather than the initial attitude with which he started his work, as has often been suggested by those who would invest the first-century Galilean prophet in the garments of a twentieth-century champion of the social gospel.

If the two contentions urged in an earlier chapter be accepted—namely, (1) that the impending kingdom, or "age to come," was essentially the apocalyptic expectation that God's long-deferred promise was to be realized in a catastrophic overthrow of the present order and the birth of a literally new age and world, and (2) that Jesus believed himself without qualification a prophet sent by God to announce this blessed event—then many seeming difficulties in need of a "common-sense" explanation vanish.

Such a proclamation would have seemed very far from "good news" to many who listened. It would have been a dangerous and radical attack upon the *status quo*. As has been already remarked, there were probably very few in Palestine who doubted the reality of the eventual dawn of the "golden age," in which God's long-deferred promise to the seed of Abraham would be gloriously realized. But the situation in which they found themselves, in the light of the experiences through which they had passed, had made them wary of any overt act or any attempt at rabble-rousing which might well thrust them out of the frying pan and into the fire.

To be sure, they were under the control of Rome. That was an outrage, at least a heavy burden to bear; but it was only one more example to which they had long become accustomed. It was God, not men—even Romans!—who was ruling. It was he who had raised up Rome and permitted her legions to be supreme, even as it had been God, not Nebuchadrezzar or Cyrus or Alexander, who had been the source of the bitter experiences of the past. It was all a part of his chastening love for his own peculiar people, perfecting them through trials which others less highborn were not called to endure. When God saw fit to end the period of testing, he would. Thus many had become accustomed to wait upon the Lord and to view with distaste any attempt to force the hand of the Almighty.

More than that, Rome's hand, though firm, was far from obtrusively heavy. Gone was the fear of interference with their religion. They were completely free to worship, to conduct their daily life in accord with what they were sure was the divinely revealed blueprint in the Scriptures. The Sanhedrin, hallowed by the years and thus fondly believed to have been established by none less than Moses himself, was the supreme native court with almost unlimited power, both legislative and executive. The Roman governor rarely interfered; for the most part he remained in the far more congenial Cæsarea, coming to Jerusalem only at times of the larger festivals. Taxes were high, but they were less burdensome than in earlier years. In able fashion Rome had corrected earlier tax abuses in her provinces. Farming out of fiscal taxes had long since been stopped. Instead they were collected by salaried government officers, whose accounts were scrupulously audited. Much of the money collected went into the improvement of the province itself—roads, harbors, buildings. The customs taxes (internal revenue), unlike the fiscal taxes, were still farmed out, and were a constant source of irritation. Not unnaturally those engaged in collecting them were cordially hated, regularly dubbed "robbers," and scornfully joined with the "sinners and harlots" in popular parlance.

Thus the actual government was largely in the hands of the native aristocracy. The Sanhedrin was presided over by the high priest. By and large, it was the real machinery of administration.

Small wonder then that those in positions of wealth and power were the most zealous in guarding against an undue rocking of the heavily laden little ship of state. Well did they know the inevitable result of revolt, however seemingly "patriotic" its intent. Thus the group commonly styled Sadducees, who seem by the time of the ministry of Jesus to have become for the most part wealthy landowners, politically prominent, and in consequence ultraconservative, would be as violently hostile to a "dangerous" figure like the prophet from Galilee as they were to any other group, notably the "home rule party," ever eager to stage a revolution and confident God would inevitably rally to their side.

Along with the Sadducees was the other group, the Pharisees. Josephus' famous characterization of them would seem entirely factual: "The Pharisees have delivered to the people a great many observances by succession from their fathers, which are not written in the law of Moses; and for that reason it is that the Sadducees reject them, and say that we [Josephus was a Pharisee] are to esteem those observances to be obligatory which are in the written word, but are not to observe what are derived from the tradition of our forefathers." [10]

[10] Josephus, *Antt.* 13, 10, 6.

To understand the basic differences, not alone between these two groups—Pharisees and Sadducees—but also of such splinter groups as the Essenes, which separated from both of them, one must realize the fundamental contention of Judaism, that in the law all of God's revealed will and requirements are to be found.

But the passing of the years had made many demands. Life in Roman Palestine was far different than in the days when the traditional law had become established and made sacrosanct. As gradually the law had become the final source of God's will and purpose, thus outmoding both the prophet and the priest, there had arisen an increasingly large group who found their greatest concern in knowing and observing God's will as thus revealed. The problem, although probably never expressed as such, was an unchanging law in a changing society. Thus those popularly known as Pharisees were attempting by their oral tradition to make the old law work in the new society. And by making explicit what they were sure was implicit in the written law—for this was in essence their prized "oral law" or tradition—of course they unconsciously read in much that they were eager to read out.

To their opponents, the Sadducees, such an action was unwarrantable. The written word was sufficient.[11] What was good enough for Moses was good enough for them. As fundamentalists in every age are wont to do, they closed their eyes to the need of change—and their well-intrenched financial position made this myopia the easier. To them the Pharisees were latitudinarians. To the Pharisees the charge seemed unwarranted. They were not reading in anything new; they

[11] The Sadducees of necessity had their tradition which amplified and made explicit the written Law, and it was often definitely more austere and rigorous than that of the Pharisees. Unlike the latter, they did not give to it the authority of the Law. It was opinion.

were simply reading out what God himself had written in as
he foresaw the developing years.

To such a group as the Essenes, and even more to the
Covenanters of Damascus, both answers were wrong. Instead
of attempting to make the old law fit the new environs, they
reversed the process and sought in their ghettos and camps
to relive the wilderness experiences of Israel. Naturally, in
this fancied and artificial "reliving" they had introduced
many notions, especially of an ascetic quality, the origin of
which is still hotly debated and disputed,[12] which were alien
to the genius of Judaism.

While it is unlikely that the majority of Pharisees were
scholars, in the sense that the scribes were—who may be
loosely styled the biblical Ph.D.'s of their time—they did
wholeheartedly accept and approve their findings. Like the
Sadducees, they regarded with intense disapprobation man-
made attempts to force the hand of God. In a word: "Let
God do it." While by and large the Pharisees may not have
had wealth to compare with that of the landowning Sadducees, they apparently constituted what may roughly be
styled the middle class, both in education and position, far
removed from the bulk of the population, and cushioned by
their position and education from many of the rigors and
rough spots so galling to those shielded neither by wealth
nor education.

It is against this background that the Galilean prophet is
to be seen. Passionately convinced that God had commis-
sioned him to sound the word, he uttered his clarion call:
"The time is fulfilled, and the kingdom of God is at hand."
And it is not difficult to understand the reception of this word.

[12] For a more detailed discussion of all these "sects" the reader is referred to my *Christian Beginnings*, pp. 111–128.

To those in authority, established and secure, it was an entirely unacceptable blast at all that seemed secure. "The axe is laid at the root of the tree" [13] is not a word likely to prove acceptable to those in authority. It cuts too close home, regardless of who is to wield the axe. For them there is no need to postulate an extended period of growing hostility. From the start this word would be anathema. So long as the prophet remained in rural Galilee and without too great a following, they might well be less concerned. As soon as he approached Jerusalem with his band of followers and uttered his blasphemy against the temple and predicted its speedy collapse, his doom was sealed.

To the educated he became increasingly obnoxious. Although theirs may not have been at the very start so intense a fear and hatred as was felt among those in positions of authority and wealth, there could not fail to be an initial suspicion. One of the most conspicuous characteristics of the rabbinical literature—Mishnah, Talmuds, and Midrashes —is their silence about all that can be styled "apocalyptic." Thus it is easy to dismiss apocalypticism from normative Judaism, and it has been not infrequently done. It is true so far as educated, literary Judaism is concerned. They studiedly ignored this wildfire literature. As the days went on, their contempt for the unlearned upstart grew more intense as his every act and pretension seemed to them not only a flagrant violation of what was proper, but a deliberate attack upon them in their devotion to what they knew was God's will for man. Why, he dared to speak for God, when every Jew *knew* that God spoke through the law! He

[13] Matt. 3:10 and Luke 3:9; cf. Matt. 7:16–20 and also Luke 6:43–44. Though this word now stands in the mouth of John the Baptist, it is highly probable, as has been already suggested, that it, like all of John's reported messages, is in essence a word of Jesus, subsequently transferred to that one's "Christianized" forerunner.

ventured to make his utterances unqualified by precedent
(which easily led to the scandalous claim, "It has been said
to them of old, but I say unto you") in such marked contrast
to their learned leaders, who habitually cited an earlier
pundit as their authority!

But there were many others to whom the clarion cry of
the prophet about the impending change was highly acceptable. To them any change must *per se* be for the better; they
had nothing to lose and everything to gain. Involved in the
daily round of trying to wrest a living for themselves and
families; confronted with taxes from which there was no
relief; regarded with contempt by their more secure fellows,
who dubbed them "sinners" because of their inability to find
the time to study and observe the endless ramifications of
the law which their betters were constantly discovering—
it is small wonder that the vision of a complete change of
economy and rule was attractive. In a word, to those at the
bottom of the wheel, whichever way the wheel were to turn,
it could not fail to bring an improvement. While in the more
highly educated circles apocalyptic thinking, together with
the literature it produced, was not popular, it was highly
acceptable to many of the *ame ha-ares*—"people of the land,"
or as we so often dub them, the common people—and they
"heard it gladly."

In this situation there could scarcely fail to be one result.
Jesus was convinced that he had been especially empowered
by God to sound the long longed-for word. In consequence,
he "knew" that he was "right," that his word was God's, not
his. However alien to our way of thinking the outlook and
self-confidence of the ancient Semitic prophet may appear,
however much we may try to dismiss it as "abnormal," nevertheless to minimize or to deny its presence in a long line of
men who passionately believed that they had been so em-

powered and—even more important—were so regarded by their fellows, this is to close our eyes to the possibility of a correct understanding of a long chapter in the history of the past.

Since Jesus was himself so passionately convinced that he had been chosen to be God's trumpet, and because he was equally convinced that the word he was compelled to sound was such good news—no longer the dreadful warning of an Amos or Jeremiah, but a call to enter the "joys of their Lord" —of course all would joyfully hear.

As the days wore on and the result of Jesus' proclamation became more and more apparent, the outcome was inevitable. Many were hearing the word and eagerly awaiting its fulfillment. But others were singularly opposed. What could be holding them back? What could be blinding their eyes to what was obviously the greatest boon in life? Whatever was holding them back, it must be evil, for it was causing men to refuse God's invitation.

Who were the ones who turned a scornful deaf ear? Those who had wealth, position, learning. Who were hearkening? The humble and the poor and the uneducated. Is it surprising that Jesus put his finger on the seemingly patent cause that in the prophet who knew he was uttering God's call, which would properly be eagerly hailed by all God's sons and daughters, opposition to wealth arose very naturally?

It is surely not surprising that under these circumstances Jesus found himself drawn closer and closer to those who accepted his—God's!—word, and who, by their following him, made evident that they were eager to obey God. It may well be that this was no essential change of front for Jesus. Certainly there is nothing in the materials at our disposal to suggest that his was an inheritance of either wealth or education. Like most in every age who are found in what is now termed the "lower economic brackets," he may well have had a background of suspicion toward the wealthy and a confidence that they were generally heartless to their less fortunate brethren, if not actually parasites. Amos and Micah stand out as earlier representatives of this view. But whatever his native inclination, the significant point is that it was the way his word was accepted that led to his appearing the understanding and sympathizing "friend of publicans and sinners," the caustic and unsympathetic foe of those in positions of wealth and power.

11

"Not as the scribes"

IN THE VARIOUS quick glimpses of the clashes of
Jesus with the Pharisees with which the gospels provide us,
one thing is certain. Never do they charge him with what
today would be styled heresy. In all respects he was seemingly a devout and orthodox Jew, with complete and unques-
tioned acceptance of and devotion to an all-wise and all-
powerful God. The claim, often made, that Jesus taught a
new conception of God, that he for the first time taught men
that God was their father and that they in consequence were
brothers, is contrary to the evidence. That that was his view
is entirely likely, but the assumption that thereby he had
broken with his ancestral religion or advanced beyond it is
quite unwarranted.

The addition of the words "in heaven" to the regular salu-
tation, "Our Father," in Jewish prayers, which has often been
cited by Christian critics [1] as an indication of the remoteness of God from his world in the thinking of Judaism at
the dawn of the Christian era, indicates nothing of the sort.
(When the phrase occurs in Christian prayers, notably at

[1] E.g., W. Bousset, *Religion des Judentums*, 2nd ed., pp. 431 f.

Matt. 6:9, [its indication of] the remoteness of the Deity is
apparently to them less marked.) The phrase simply serves
to remove any possible ambiguity between God and an
earthly father. It does not indicate any new conception or
stress any new relationship. Orthodox Judaism never has had
a "doctrine of God." Rather it simply accepted him. Thus the
phrase is not theological but a characteristic expression of
piety. A thoughtful examination of the Jewish literature of
devotion, its spontaneous and natural ascription to God of
all the virtues and attitudes—even the humblest—which men
were enjoined to have and show, will dispel any suspicion
that it was a revolutionary insight of Jesus which brought
God back from his earlier remoteness and regarded him as
a father to be loved because he first loved us, not as an
"oriental potentate" before whom men must grovel.[2] To
the lavish collection of passages, easily available for the inter-
ested reader, which makes so obvious the spontaneous and
unstudied piety of Israel, may be added one of haunting
charm. In commenting upon Exod. 14:19 ("The angel of
God, who went before the camp of Israel, removed and went
behind them") R. Judah ben Ila'i remarked:

A rich verse the idea of which is found in many places. . . . It is
like a man who was walking on the way and letting his son go on
before him; came robbers in front to take the boy captive, the
father put him behind him; came a wolf from behind, he put him
in front; came robbers in front and wolves behind, he took him
up in his arms; did he begin to be troubled by the heat of the sun,
his father stretched his own garment over him; was he hungry,
he gave him food, thirsty, he gave him to drink. Just so God did,
as it is written . . . : He led Israel, his son, and took it in his arms
[Hos. 11:1–2]; spread over it a cloud to shelter it from the heat

---

[2] See my *Christian Beginnings*, pp. 99–104; and for a full and thoroughly
documented statement, G. F. Moore, *Judaism*, II, pp. 201–211—*magister
meus et amicus*.

[Ps. 105:39]; fed it with bread from heaven [Exod. 16:4]; brought streams out of the rock for it to drink [Ps. 78:16]; God has compassion as a father on his sons [Ps. 103:13]; and comforts like a mother [Isa. 66:13].[3]

This was the sort of piety in which Jesus was brought up and of which the Gospel of Matthew provides so faithful a picture.

Nor was it otherwise with the other great insistence of Israel, the sanctity and completeness of the Scriptures. That Jesus actually said: "Think not that I came to destroy the law or the prophets: I came not to destroy, but to fulfil. For verily I say unto you, Till heaven and earth pass away, one jot or one tittle shall in no wise pass away from the law, till all things be accomplished," [4] is unlikely, not because it expresses a view repugnant to him, but rather because it is inconceivable that he could have felt it necessary to utter such a truism.

But it was precisely at this point, his completely orthodox veneration for the law and prophets, that he seems to have come into conflict with the religious leaders, the scribes and Pharisees, and for two basic reasons: first, because he was—that is, believed himself to be—a prophet; and second, because he was a layman.

It has long been a popular Christian commonplace that the Pharisees misunderstood Jesus. It is far more rarely recognized that he may well have misunderstood them. As has already been urged, to understand the real nature of Judaism one must recognize the basic fact that Judaism had come to regard its Scripture—the "law and the prophets"— as the complete and all-inclusive revelation of God, in which

[3] Pesiḳta ed. Buber 139a, quoted by Moore, *op. cit.*, II, pp. 203 f.
[4] Matt. 5:17 f.

every last detail of life, as it was and as it would be, stood anticipated and provided for. But this revelation was so succinctly expressed that at times it was implicit and superficially obscure. Only by study could it be discerned. Naturally, the average man, untrained in the schools and faced with the problem of wresting a livelihood from what was at best a far from easy land, did not have either the time or ability to become proficient in this unlocking of the Scriptures.

Nonetheless, whatever the difficulties involved, nothing could compare in the eyes of the devout with this procedure. The Scripture was God's revelation, and it was his injunction that all men obey it. To obey it, one must know it. Thus, in sober fact, ignorance was no excuse. Nothing could compare in importance with this divinely required obligation. Furthermore, the obligation was not laid by a capricious tyrant, from whose unreasonable demands it was proper to attempt to escape. It was laid by God, the all-loving Father, for the blessing and benefit of his especially beloved children. Thus on every ground, failure to keep the law, the readiness to allow any other interests or demands to interpose, was to flout the Father; in a word, to say "I won't" to the demand, "Son, work in the vineyard." Furthermore, in theory, there was no gradation of sin in these matters. All flouting of God's will was fatal.

Hence it is not surprising that, in the eyes of the pious, keeping the law in all its detail was all-important. Those who failed—whatever their alleged excuses—were "sinners." Consequently, in Judaism the true aristocracy was not of wealth but of learning. Even the priests, if they were not learned in the matter of expounding the law—and most of them were not—were regarded by the Pharisees as "sinners" and violators of God's will, for they were allowing other concerns to obscure their prime responsibility.

Thus in addition to the elementary schools, to be found in every village, in which children learned their ABC's (with the Scriptures, naturally, their textbook), were higher schools in which students and teachers sought to find and make available the "kidney-fat of wheat" and the "blood of the grape," [5] that is, to make explicit and usable what was implicit and often obscure. Through the generations had arisen the oral interpretation, which was passed on from teacher to pupil and which eventually came to be written down to form the core of what we know today as the Rabbinical Literature. The ideal student was the one who, like a carefully plastered cistern, retained without losing a drop what was poured in. Of necessity the normal form of teaching was in terms of citing what had been uttered by this worthy or that, not new pronouncements unsupported by precedent.

An anecdote told of none less than the eminent teacher Hillel well reveals this habitual practice. In a remote village a perplexing problem had arisen as to the proper procedure when the fourteenth of Nisan fell upon a Sabbath. Was the obligation to slaughter and prepare the victim for next day's Passover superior to those which expressly forbade all labor on the Sabbath? In this quandary the villagers were

---

[5] By these descriptive terms were indicated the two sorts of material in the "unwritten law," which the world knows as the Rabbinical Literature: the *Halakah*, literally, the "rule to go by," that is, the legal material, minutely discussed in what often appears a hypercritical manner; and the *Haggadah*, the exposition of those parts of the Scriptures not primarily legal, but of a sort to allow an imaginative development of thoughts suggested by the text. Nor was this latter homiletic material minimized. It was a rabbinic commonplace: "If you would learn to know Him at whose word the world came into being, learn Haggadah, for by this means you will come to know the Holy One and cleave to his ways."

advised to consult the learned teacher Hillel. Patiently he
sought by three lines of argument to prove that the legisla-
tion for the proper observance of the Passover prevailed.
In contempt the villagers retorted: "What could we expect
from a Babylonian!" But when after a fruitless day of arguing
he fell back on tradition: "Thus I heard it from Shemaiah
and Abtalion," not only did their opposition cease, but they
elected him their president.[6]

It is against this backdrop that the amazed word charac-
terizing Jesus' proclamation is to be understood: "The multitudes were astonished at his teaching: for he taught them as
one having authority, and not as their scribes." [7] No appeal
to precedent; instead an unqualified pronouncement. Of
course it was amazing to his hearers; but to the prophet himself it was perfectly natural. He was not a teacher, was not
arguing, was not attempting to balance arguments. Instead
he was uttering the word God had put in his mouth. It was
not his reasoning which he was trying to defend; it was God's
clarion call, which he as his herald was announcing. It might
seem strange to his hearers; it would have seemed entirely
natural to an Amos, a Hosea, or a Jeremiah.

To those who were becoming increasingly scandalized by
his insistent word, who viewed it with contempt and growing concern, it was the irresponsible raving of an ignorant
and mad fanatic in the clutches of evil demons. To those to
whom his word was acceptable and who were thus disposed
to accept him at his own valuation, this amazing independence, this "speaking with authority," without appeal to precedent, which none of them would dream of venturing, was but
an additional proof of his claim. How else would he venture
so unheard-of an independence and authority!

<hr />

[6] Jer. Pesaḥim 33a; Pesaḥim 66a.   [7] Matt. 7:28 f.

There is another important aspect to this picture which has been regularly overlooked or else distorted. This has to do with the nature and purpose of the rapidly increasing "oral tradition," which sought to make explicit what was believed to be implicit. By Christian readers this has been viewed as casuistry and hair-splitting, the heartless attempt to burden the poor and the pious with unnecessary and crippling restrictions: "Count that day lost whose low-descending sun finds no new 'must' which simply can't be done." Thus the term *Pharisee* has easily come to suggest the arrogant, unlovely deviser of burdens to be cast upon the hapless poor, and which the deviser, despite his pious-sounding voice, has no slightest intent to bear himself—in a word "hypocrite!"

And it must be confessed that there is much in the gospel record which evidences this appraisal. Moreover, it is highly likely that in this estimate Jesus himself concurred: "They bind heavy burdens and grievous to be borne, and lay them on men's shoulders; but they themselves will not move them with their finger." [8] "Full well [beautifully!] do ye reject the commandment of God, that ye may keep your tradition." [9] I see little reason to question that these bitter words of criticism reflect very accurately the attitude of Jesus, as they do that of hundreds of his followers, and that they were a strictly honest protest against what to him seemed an unwarranted and perverse violation of the written law for their own purposes.

It may very well be that there were many contemporary Pharisees of harsh and unlovely disposition who merited this tongue-lashing, precisely as there are unfortunately many Christians today who can make the ways of God seem highly repellent. But this was nonetheless not the genius of Phari-

[8] Matt. 23:4; cf. Luke 11:46. [9] Mark 7:9.

saism, and the sorry specimen held up to contempt in Luke 18:9–14 is as far from being a true representative of it as are the many pseudo-Christians today who seemingly evidence so complete a lack of understanding of the religion which they claim to admire and embrace.

The aim of the Pharisee was to make possible the observance of the Law, not the reverse; that is, the attempt was to adapt the old law to the new ways and demands that the passing centuries had entailed. But such a statement would have scandalized him. With the belief that all that ever was to happen was in God's mind from the earliest beginning, the answer was, of course, actually present in the law. He was not reading anything new in; rather he was making clear what was already there.

"Remember the Sabbath day to keep it holy" is easily said. But how did this apply in Jerusalem? Work was eschewed; but what was work? Through the years the seemingly finespun distinction as to what was, what was not, within the strict limit of two thousand cubits, the maximum permitted for a Sabbath day's journey; the extreme fussiness about the ceremonial washing of hands—these have seemed to many modern men both absurd and a needless burden, the apogee of an arid legalism. This fails to see that the object was to preserve and make viable ancient laws, which unmodified would have been utterly impossible. Thus by interpreting "place" in the ancient adage, "Abide ye every man in his *place;* let no man go out of his place on the seventh day" (Exod. 16:29), as *city,* not the man's *house,* he was permitted to cross the whole city and then continue the extra two thousand cubits. Certainly the washing of hands, against which so much thoughtless criticism has been raised, was a vast deal easier and less demanding than that for which it was an interpretation; viz., cleansing of the whole body and ⟩

the lapse of time until sunset. In a word—and these examples are but two of many—the attempt was to make possible the keeping of an ancient law designed for circumstances utterly different from those with which men were now confronted. Far from adding to the rigors of the law, the attempt was just the reverse. Small wonder that to real literalists, as the ascetic sects with their continual insistence, "To your tents, O Israel," the Pharisees were gross latitudinarians.

Whether theirs was the ideal solution or not, from the point of view of modern Americans, who view laws as the product of human and often venal lawmakers, is of no consequence. What is important is that in the view of the Pharisee his was the only possible course of action, a practice hallowed by an endless series of generations from Moses to the present day. Thus, when one who in their eyes was an ignorant nobody sought to inveigh against this ancient practice and to charge them with seeking to annul God's changeless law, when they knew their intent was the reverse, it spelled trouble. On the other hand, to a layman like Jesus it was easy and natural to lose sight of the object, the aim of their endeavors, and to see only the innovations, many of the values of which were to him remote.

A reasonably close parallel is to be seen in the annoyance with which the modern layman regards many legal niceties. Here is a man whom everybody—judge, jurors, and lawyers —knows is guilty; but because the foolproof evidence was legally inadmissible, the criminal goes free. But when the layman protests to his friend, a trained lawyer, he is apt to receive a pitying smile for his stupidity in failing to see that without these safeguards human rights would be endangered.

There were undoubtedly many abuses in first-century Palestine—Galilee as well as Jerusalem—and surely frequently these "innovations" proved in practice not only meaningless but at times a real burden. The point here is that it was inevitable that a deep gulf should have stood between one like Jesus and the scribes and their supporters. Had the latter found the prophet's word acceptable, the prophet might well have failed to be repulsed by their practices, even as he failed to be repulsed by the practices of the "sinners" who hearkened with eagerness. And had the Pharisees been able to find his message congenial and his clarion call tolerable, they would have been quite able to discover both him and his message in the all-inclusive Scripture.

12

"Is not this the carpenter?"

I N VIEW OF the popular notion of Jesus as primarily a teacher, and thus of necessity an interpreter of the law, the question has seemed natural: Did he not tend to relax its strictures? Does not his attitude to the Sabbath, which, if the many gospel stories are to be trusted, was highly scandalous in the eyes of the orthodox, seem so to suggest? On the other hand, his unqualified opposition to divorce,[1] quite in contrast to prevailing practice, and his insistence that the innovation permitted by Moses was prompted by the people's "hardness of heart"[2] and in flat violation of God's agelong decree, might seem to indicate greater severity.

---

[1] The qualifying clause, "save for the cause of fornication," twice inserted by Matthew (5:32 and 19:9) is a palpable addition, in direct contradiction of the tradition preserved by Paul (I Cor. 7:10–11), Mark (10:11–12), Luke (16:18), and for the purpose of making an uncompromising and impossible teaching more workable in a society which seemed perversely determined to last, at least for a season. Note also a similar change in the story of the Rich Ruler. Mark's unqualified "One thing thou lackest" (10:21) has been softened by Matthew into a counsel of perfection, "If thou wouldest be perfect" (19:21).

[2] Mark 10:2–12.

Both of these instances would seem but additional proof of what must be styled Jesus' essentially "lay approach." That is, he failed to see—or if he saw, to be favorably impressed by the fact—that the real purpose of the religious leaders was to make the law workable. In his eyes they were constantly "rejecting the commandment of God" to keep their own traditions. This was both wrong and unnecessary.

In this appraisal, "wrong and unnecessary," we come to the heart of the matter. Jesus' conviction that the end of the present age was at hand dominated all his thinking. He was not talking to a group of men in a world long to last and aiding them the better to meet its demands. Rather he saw the end of all these abuses and therewith of all need of these man-made compromises and changes.

The consistent tone and undercurrent in his reported "teaching" is clear once we concede this seemingly certain fact. There are many examples. The unqualified word to the Rich Ruler: Since the only pearl of price is admittance to the fast-approaching kingdom, divest yourself of everything which blinds your eyes to it. "If any man would go to law with thee, and take away thy coat, let him have thy cloak also"; [3] "Resist not him that is evil"; [4] "Give to him that asketh"; [5] "Turn the other cheek." [6] These precepts are readily repeated and regularly applauded with little thought of the evil effect upon an on-going society such easy avoidance of responsibility must eventually entail. But in the thinking of the man who so unqualifiedly announced them life was not to continue as it was. A completely new and different sort of life was speedily to dawn.

Thus the repeated attempts through the years to make this seeming instruction sound practical in a world and society

[3] Matt. 5:40.   [4] Matt. 5:39.   [5] Matt. 5:42.
[6] Matt. 5:39.

which are expected to continue—the attempts to see in
Jesus the proponent of what has come to be styled "the
social gospel"—result in an entire misunderstanding of the
prophet from Nazareth.

His demand that the Rich Ruler sell all that he had was
not for the purpose of aiding the poor from the distributed
bounty. It was an imperative necessity for the man himself,
were he to be ready for the speedily dawning day. So Jesus'
other insistences. Attempts to water them down into pleasant
admonitions to be generous and even-tempered are far from
impressive. To repeat, the demands are regularly for the sake
of the man himself, not for the alleviation and betterment
of society and the world at large. The world and its society
were speedily to pass, and a new and totally other age was
to dawn. And this change was to be brought about by God,
not by social engineers.

Not infrequently this has been recognized, in part. An
older type of ultraorthodox preachers looked askance at any
attempt to read a social gospel into Jesus' mission and concern. Thus far they were undoubtedly correct. They failed
to see, however, that Jesus' emphasis was based upon the
conviction of the near approach of the end, and that for us
to continue his insistence in a world view where the original
basic postulates are no longer accepted is hopeless, if not
perverse.

For many who held—as many still do—this view of a
speedy end the problem seemed less acute. Millennialists,
both pre- and post-, with their expectation of the end, which
they have come to see in terms of a bodily return of Jesus,
may well believe that they are interpreting him with strict
literalness—as in actual fact they are, save for their certainty that Jesus had expected and promised such a personal
return. The difficulty lies not in their understanding of this

aspect of history, but in their failure to see its impossibility today. That Jesus had expected the immediate end is certain. Equally certain it is that in this expectation he was sorely mistaken.

Here lies the nub of the difficulty. It is so hard to permit one whom love and reverence have made an eternal figure to hold views which we have come to see are impossible! Thus the one group insists that Jesus could not be mistaken, that the time must and will come, and speedily. Others, to whom this whole matter of the end of the world is grotesquely impossible, find it equally difficult to admit that Jesus was wrong. So they seek to free him from the onus of having held views which to them are at best quixotic.

Both attempts are not only wrong but wrongheaded. The one fails to see that in Jesus' thinking the end was imminent, would come in his generation. Instead, through the centuries they have been sure that it would come in *their* generation, and that each previous generation had been inexact in its computation of the end. Others, to whom the whole apocalyptic view is a vast mistake, fail to see that to an earlier generation, notably first-century Judaism, expectations which in modern eyes seem fantastic, if not insane, might well be natural and reasonable. In brief, they refuse to allow a first-century Jew to think like a first-century Jew, and instead seek to view him as a social engineer, engrossed with slum clearance and proper race relations. Both groups, though independently and each with contempt for the other, seek to do what mankind has through the centuries sought to do with God, viz., make him in their own image. And while the Christ of faith is docile in their hands, the Jesus of history entirely eludes them.

The retort is easy, and it has been frequently made, as it was so bitterly to Albert Schweitzer, in the days before he

had become the Christian saint and universal idol: This re-
duces the teaching of Jesus to the status of an interim ethic,
significant only temporarily during the wait for the dawning
kingdom.

To a degree the charge is correct, although it seems to me
more accurate to style it a "kingdom ethic" rather than an
"interim ethic." This was the way that men—those fortunate
enough to be admitted to the kingdom—would live in the
new age and the new world. In the "interim" before the
kingdom dawned they must have adopted the sort of conduct they would continue to follow in the blessed new age.
It may very well be that in the eyes of Jesus there was nothing radically new in such a way of life. Rather, it was the
way man had lived in their earlier innocence before they
had allowed themselves by their new traditions to vitiate
and change the ways ordained by God.[7]

Surely such an assumption as to Jesus' view in this regard
is in strict accord with what we know of the Semitic world's
confidence in the persistence of all that is—or ever has been
under the blessing of God. To us the eighth-century prophets—Amos, Hosea, Micah—seem radical innovators with
their ethical demands and their contempt for age-old sacrifice. But the prophets thought themselves far from being
innovators. Instead they were calling the nation back to the
good old days and ways. Sacrifice was in their eyes invented
by man, not ordained by God. The conduct which God was
demanding now he had always insisted upon.

So Jesus. Men were to repent of their evil practices. That
meant they were to stop doing them, for repentance was a

[7] There is no indication in the gospels and certainly little probability
that Jesus attempted to outline in any detail, as would a modern teacher
of systematic ethics, precisely what this "sort of conduct" entailed. It was, of
course, to be found in the all-encompassing law when the latter was read
with the eyes of trusting obedience and "not as the scribes."

thing of doing. Henceforth they were to live as God had in
the beginning ordained they should. In the last analysis, it
would seem that for Jesus the ideal life, which God had
ordained from the beginning and which would be demanded
by his final judge at the coming Final Judgment, was the
sort of life and conduct which appealed to him personally.

To many this may seem an overeasy and subjective dis-
missal of a problem hotly debated through the years. Nonetheless it would appear to me very difficult to find a more
basic and universally evidenced standard or, as many love
to style it, *norm* of conduct.

And this direct, "common sense" approach, free from any
attempt at support from precedent, may not only have added
freshness and force to his words but also have seemed ex-
plicable only in terms of his own claim: it was God, not he,
who was speaking. When charged by his opponents that he
was inspired by the power of evil—of Satan; not God, as he
claimed—his answer was novel: Behold the results. Are they
good or bad? If the former, how can they be the product of
one who is unqualifiedly evil? [8] To the charge that he spent
too much time with "publicans and sinners," again the direct
and common-sense retort: It is the sick, not the well, who
need a physician.[9]

Throughout those words which now stand attributed to
Jesus and which seem relatively free from revision and re-
working, there is a constant down-to-earth and homespun
quality of practical common sense. They show an entirely
unstudied and unembarrassed stress on the very practical
advantage to the man so acting. "Judge not!" Why? Because
it is not in accord with the highest ethical norms, that is, because it is wrong, or even because it is forbidden by God? No
indeed. If you don't judge, you will not be judged. To stretch

---

[8] Mark 3:22 ff.   [9] Mark 2:17.

and burlesque this to mean that Jesus was indifferent to what God had said in the all-embracing law or that it evidences a studied and mercenary *quid pro quo* motive for action is absurd. But one cannot read these words—and the score of others like them—without the impression that they come from a man who is accustomed to a direct and common-sense view of what is "obviously" fair and sensible and who is equally accustomed to express himself in the homeliest and simplest way. This is what I mean by styling Jesus a layman. How far removed such plain expression is from the studied and balanced reflection of the "careful scholar," who is ever guarding himself from academic rebuke for venturing to talk the simple, direct language of men! Of course the common people heard him gladly; equally unsurprising is the hostility that this aroused in those whose outlook and training made them suspicious of common sense and certain that it was at best shallow, if not perverse.

It is needless to multiply these examples. To me they go far toward illumining what has seemed to so many a baffling enigma: precisely what was it that led an increasingly large group to see in him a man sent by God? To attempt to find the answer in any one specific aspect is to court failure. What is styled his "message," that is, his teaching, is far from unique. His birth and upbringing would seem quite in the ordinary pattern. Surely there were many who were convinced that the end was at hand, many others whose ways of life led to the belief that they were swayed by powers not their own.

That the whole is far larger than the sum of its parts—at least, its easily discernible parts—may seem a truism. It can be, nonetheless, profoundly true. And to the historian, viewing an occasional figure in the pages of the past who seems to have towered over his fellows, yet possessing little which analysis can fasten on as "unique," there is but one course. Even though he may not be able to explain *why* this figure or that "caught on," while hundreds of others through the years, whose outward careers seem so similar, passed on with little apparent result, he cannot but admit that occasionally it did happen.

This is not to be forgotten when we seek to view Jesus of Nazareth. To me the only explanation of the tremendous effect he had upon his contemporaries is to be found in that amazing and baffling congeries of gifts and abilities which we call "personality." Jesus was able to convince many among whom he moved that he was what he believed himself to be. In crude terms, he "sold himself."

Given the time and the place, there could be but one result. Once men were convinced that God had sent him, had given him that message, a message which was momentarily to be fulfilled, nothing else could matter. He was crucified. His enemies had triumphed? Indeed they had not! Every prophet of the past had died, most of them at the hands of their foes. But nonetheless they had been right. Their message was speedily verified by God himself, despite the actions of wicked and sin-blinded men. So for Jesus. Since it was God's word, it too must be realized.

Unlike so many of the prophets of old whose word was doom, this prophet had announced the momentary dawn of Israel's long-awaited triumph and blessed release. And he had convinced many that the one great demand was to ready themselves for the dawn of this wondrous Day. He was put to death. But this could not quench the movement. He had never claimed that he was to inaugurate the Day. His rôle had been to announce it. Thus his death, far from invalidating his message, had but made more sure his prophetic claim. They found themselves unable to free themselves of his presence. Once again, there is a truth, not to be escaped, in the "power of an endless life." He had built himself and his dream so completely into many who had been with him through the months that any momentary fears and disillusion which the bleak Friday on Golgotha had aroused had to vanish. Of course they "saw" him again amid the familiar scenes by Galilee's lake—"saw" him as he had electrified his groups of listeners, had strangely quieted men possessed of devils, had had time to comfort a grief-stricken mother, had flamed forth his contempt for the high and mighty whose hands were heavy. There is little need of wandering into the strange arcana, contrary to all we think we know of an orderly universe, and postulating magical changes on a tired and broken body. The real Easter miracle was not a changed Jesus but changed disciples. And that was a change they could not escape.

The real Jesus was not put in any garden tomb. His battered body, yes; but it would be very crass and shortsighted to attempt to appraise Jesus, or any other man or woman, in terms of what is to be measured by a pair of hospital scales or glimpsed by a candid camera. The qualities, essence, or whatever other terms be used to attempt to classify and interpret "personality," quite elude the scales and camera. But it is they which constitute the real person, and it is they which constituted the real Jesus. And *this* was not put into any grave. It had been built by that strange alchemy of life into those with whom he had been in contact. Had this not been the case, it is highly unlikely that they would have "seen" him in the days following Easter.

13

"Whose son is he?"
The son of David?

Few questions regarding Jesus have been more
continually and heatedly debated through the years than that
of the authority he claimed for himself. Reduced to simplest
terms this controversy has involved two questions: Did he
claim to be the "Son of David"? Did he claim to be the "Son
of man"? Reasons have already been indicated in these
pages, which, if accepted, would seem to require an unqualified *no* to both queries. That Jesus claimed authority
for himself cannot be doubted. But the evidence certainly
seems to suggest that this authority was the authority of a
prophet of God, appointed by God to herald the speedy
dawn of the kingdom.

That Jesus would have felt the Aramaic word underlying
its Greek translation *christos* appropriate would seem to be
without question. But the word was, as was suggested in
a earlier chapter,[1] still an adjective, the precise equivalent
of the English adjective (which is its proper translation),

[1] See pp. 54 f.

130

anointed; and connoted to the Jew what is understood by our
ordained, appointed, chosen, designated. It was still far from
being a noun, the title of one specific figure designated for
one special function, namely, to lead Israel's reconvened
armies and to ascend David's throne to reign as his final and
greatest successor. In a word, the adjective *mashiah* had not
become the noun *Messiah.* In the decades subsequent to the
crucifixion this development was to take place, and eventually this new meaning for an old word was to be seen by the
subsequent followers of Jesus as one of the many titles
rightly his. Actually it was this identification which was to
prevent Christians, a hundred years later, from following Bar
Cochba in the latter's ill-omened revolt against Rome in the
days of Hadrian. For Bar Cochba had made the claim to be
the long-expected Messiah, Son of David and Israel's national and military savior. Bar Cochba seems to have been
the first in Jewish history to lay definite claim to this title
in the sense of the regal successor to David. By the unfortunate habit of many historians to apply "Messiah" and "Son
of David" loosely to every would-be leader who sought to
rebel or hamper Roman authority, this whole problem has
been sadly confused.

All this is a century after Calvary and far removed from
the one who died on one of its crosses. There is nothing in
the gospels which by any sober criticism can be regarded
as primitive and reflecting the outlook of Jesus of Nazareth
which suggests any toying by him with any such matters. It
has long been one of the few universally accepted facts that
in the Synoptic gospels, despite the views of their authors,
the regular subject of Jesus' utterance was the kingdom, not
himself the king. The Gospel of John reverses this emphasis
and portrays Jesus as habitually engaged in long sermons,
the burden of which is a series of "I am this," and "I am that."

But even in this gospel there is no hint of such a claim as
"I am the long-expected Davidic king." In the direct claim
to be "the Messiah," which this author puts in Jesus' mouth
in answer to the word of the Samaritan woman (4:25 f.), the
context suggests that the function of this figure is that of a
revealer who will teach, not of a king who will lead armies
and reign.

Earlier critics recognized the absence of any such claims
by the historic Jesus, but because of the mistaken belief that
the notion of a soon-to-come Davidic Messiah was the all-
important, all-else-eclipsing hope in the days of Jesus, they
found themselves compelled to toy with the notion that,
while such a program was alien and unwelcome to Jesus, he
was forced to lay claim to the title in order to gain a hearing,
with the hope of wooing his hearers to give up their understanding of what it involved and to accept his totally different view. The assumption that in the days of Jesus this
was the one all-important concern now being recognized
as unwarranted, there would seem little to demand that Jesus
indulged in this questionable logomachy. = war of words.

That Jesus was in the slightest concerned with the re-
establishment of David's throne would seem most unlikely.
The famous story of the awkward position into which his
opponents forced him by their cleverly cruel question: "Is it
lawful to give tribute unto Cæsar, or not?" [2] is very revealing, and should be definitive as an answer to the question,
Did Jesus claim to be the Messiah?

As is true of many other awkward stories, great ingenuity
has been shown in trying to make obscure what is crystal-
clear. Surely there is little to indicate that Jesus sought to
circumvent his hecklers by a cleverly ambiguous answer. Instead, his reply was perfectly clear: "Pay the taxes." The

[2] Mark 12:14.

question had been skillfully phrased so that whatever his answer was it would be costly. If he had said, "No, do not pay them," he could have been arrested and convicted of political treason. If his answer was, "Yes, pay them," this would be construed as an expression of unpatriotic toadying to the alien ruler.

It is not unlikely that the awkward question was more than a bit of casual heckling. By his answer Jesus definitely repudiated the position of that group of superpatriots—the 100 percenters, or as Josephus styles them, the "fourth philosophy." That this group, ever striving to force the little land into war with Rome, had seen in the prophet, who had aroused such keen interest and devotion by his revolutionary pronouncement, a very valuable ally, if not an actually highly desirable leader, is far from improbable. And their support would have been an additional safeguard for Jesus against his enemies: his arrest and suppression would have been increasingly awkward, if not impossible, without riots and bloodshed. And this the authorities feared, for well did they know the consequences: instant action by the Roman governor and very costly curtailing of their own powers of control. The one thing Rome would not tolerate was anarchy or uprising in her frontier provinces. When and if such arose, the velvet glove was stripped off and the hand of steel became evident.

There is no reason to think Jesus unaware of the consequence of his answer. Thus to those who would see in Jesus a self-recognized "Messiah," this incident is no mean stumbling block. Nor does it stand alone. His repeated words against retaliation and violence, as the much quoted "All they that take the sword shall perish with the sword," [3] (which have not infrequently been misconstrued as pro-

³ Matt. 26:52.

nouncements in favor of pacifism) may well have been directed at precisely this group of patriots.

Nor is the basic reason for Jesus' attitude hard to see. It is quite unnecessary to view him as either a pacifist or a Quisling. Rather it is but part of his "thoroughgoing eschatology." Preparation to enter the fast-approaching kingdom, this and this alone was the pearl of price. In comparison, all else paled. In the short interim, what matter who controlled Israel! At any moment the end would come, and kings, be they Cæsar or David, would vanish. Were men to be concerned with revolution and armed combat, their fate would be like that of the five foolish maidens who slumbered and slept. While thus engaged, the bridegroom might well arrive and the door be thereafter shut. The wise man would allow nothing to engage his attention. "Watch therefore: for ye know not when the lord of the house cometh, whether at even, or at midnight, or at cockcrowing, or in the morning; lest coming suddenly he find you sleeping. And what I say unto you I say unto all, Watch." [4]

When once this all-important "basic concern" of Jesus is recognized, the picture becomes clear and consistent, and the need of toning down hard sayings as "oriental hyperbole" vanishes. And so do such modern problems as his basic socio-ethical and contemporary political outlook. When one is frantically rushing to catch a train which is ready to depart, nothing else is of consequence. If, as he races toward the station, a coatless beggar grabs his overcoat, he has no time either to prevent its loss by force or to engage in a session of teaching regarding property rights, the difference between *mihi* and *tibi*. While he is arguing or struggling, the train may depart. He will wisely let the coat slip, not because of any pang of conscience because he has several suits, the beggar none, but because he cannot be delayed.

[4] Mark 13:35–37.

Attempts to see in Jesus the champion of a social gospel, shared wealth, and the other pleasing qualities and attitudes so dear today in the eyes of the socially concerned, are doomed to failure. He refuses to don our clothes or share our ideas, for he lived in the first, not the twentieth century. His concern was not to better a world which was long to last; instead it was to cause men to await a cataclysm in which the present world and all its concerns—mostly due to man's strange neglect of God's providence—would vanish, and a new utopia emerge.

Thus attempts to see the historical Jesus in the rôle of the "expected Son of David," either wholeheartedly, as did Reimarus [5] or Seeley,[6] or with reluctance and with the intent of wooing his hearers from their lower to his higher ideals, as Bousset [7] among many others insisted, are foredoomed to failure. In Jesus' dream of the future, sons of David seemingly had no especial place.

Nor is it at all certain that he was in any real sense of the lineage of David. By the time the gospels of Matthew and Luke appeared this assumption had become a firm Christian belief. In both birth stories, not to mention the artificial and mutually exclusive genealogies, this note was now being pressed, for "anointed" was no longer seen as an adjective but a specific title which demanded Davidic descent. It is possible that as early as the time of Paul a similar assumption

[5] *Von dem Zwecke Jesu und seiner Jünger,* as published by G. E. Lessing in the anonymous so-called Wolfenbüttel Fragments. H. S. Reimarus was properly regarded by Schweitzer as the pioneer in the serious "quest of the historical Jesus" (*Von Reimarus zu Wrede*).

[6] *Ecco Homo.* This highly important, although now long outdated, volume was published anonymously in 1866, much to the embarrassment of many English ecclesiastics, who were regarded as its probable author. It was subsequently avowed by Sir John Robert Seeley, at the time of its composition a professor of Latin at University College, London, but subsequently a professor of history at Cambridge.

[7] W. Bousset, *Jesus.*

had been reached, although it is conceivable that Paul's oft-quoted word, "who was born of the seed of David according to the flesh," [8] is simply an insistence that Jesus was a man, and more than that, a Jew by birth, and at the same time an unconscious reflection of Paul's pride in his own better-than-ordinary Jewish blood.[9]

It is very hard to escape the feeling that the passage in Mark, in which Jesus is made to challenge the view of the scribes that "the Christ is the son of David" and to evidence its improbability by a piece of "rabbinical casuistry" ("David himself calleth him Lord; and whence is he his son?") [10] is primitive in essence. It may also evidence an early Christian answer to the Jewish gibe: "He cannot be the anointed, for he is not of Davidic lineage," by the counter-retort: "Davidic lineage is far from being a *sine qua non.*"

Both Matthew [11] and Luke [12] retain this Markan passage, but their interpretation of it, "He is not only David's son but David's Lord," is certainly far from the Markan meaning. Indeed it may well be that it was in part due to the desire to "correct Mark" at this point that they both prefixed birth stories and genealogies in which the Davidic ancestry was almost overconspicuously insisted upon.

At our remove this matter of lineal descent is at best uncertain and debatable. Nonetheless the evidence would seem to warrant the conclusion that Jesus was apparently utterly uninterested in the matter of a re-establishment of David's throne, and never dreamed of aspiring to mount it himself.

---

[8] Rom. 1:3.

[9] Cf. "of the tribe of Benjamin" (Phil. 3:5), i.e., one of the two tribes which remained loyal to the house of David at the defection led by Rehoboam.

[10] Mark 12:35–37.   [11] Matt. 22:41–46.   [12] Luke 20:41–44.

14

"Whose son is he?"
The son of man?

THAT THE PHRASE "son of man," in its Aramaic
equivalent, was often on Jesus' lips would seem highly probable although occasionally denied. What he meant by the
words, however, has been hotly debated.

One thing is very certain. The term in English is, like the
Greek underlying it, most misleading, for the Semitic term
(in Hebrew *ben adam,* in Aramaic *bar nasha*) simply meant
man in the generic sense of the Latin *homo,* the Greek
ἄνθρωπος. Examples in the Old Testament are abundant:

> "What is man, that thou art mindful of him?
> And the son of man, that thou visitest him?" [1]

The synonymous parallelism of the two verses, so characteristic of Hebrew poetry, makes obvious the identity of "man"
in the first verse and "son of man" in the second. In Ezekiel
the term stands eighty-nine times as a vocative to the
prophet: "Son of man, stand upon thy feet." [2] To Daniel is

---

[1] Psalm 8:4.   [2] Ezek. 2:1.

the similar injunction: "Understand, O son of man; for the vision belongeth to the time of the end."[3] One more of the many examples at hand must suffice:

> "God is not a man, that he should lie,
> Neither the son of man, that he should repent."[4]

In no sense is the term filial, as might be suggested by the rendering "son of." A proper translation, as already stated, would have been *homo, ἄνθρωπος, man;* but with the tendency that translators so often exhibit to translate words, not ideas, the overliteral rendering resulted.

The matter is still further complicated. In the book of Daniel, the earliest of our full-dress apocalypses, and a writing which was to have a great influence on subsequent thinking and writing, in a vision granted to Daniel, after the passing of the several awesome beasts, representing the evil and doomed foreign nations, he sees "one like unto a son of man,"[5] who represents the kingdom of the holy people of the Most High. The imagery is crystal-clear. In contrast to the grotesque and malformed beasts which symbolize the wicked nations, Israel is seen as a *man,* the highest form of all, for it is the image of God himself.

It is very possible that we can go a step farther. These beasts which Daniel "sees" may well be the supernatural creatures whose activities in heaven—in good standard apocalyptic thinking—were so sorely affecting affairs on earth. Thus behind Israel, represented in contradistinction to the beasts as a "man," may well have been present, in the mind of the writer, a "heavenly representative." At any rate, the term *bar nasha,* "son of man"—in the capitalized sense, "The Man"—came eventually to be used as the title of the supernatural figure who was expected to appear at the time

of the end, both to inaugurate the Final Judgment and to
preside over it. To those familiar with Iranian thought will
at once occur the figure Shaoshyant, mentioned on an earlier
page, whose rôle this was. That is, it would seem probable
that by the time of Jesus, when the phrase "Son of man"
was used as an apocalyptic title ("The Man") it had replaced
this older Iranian equivalent. So the term is constantly used
in such apocalypses as Enoch and IV Ezra, and the demon-
strative "that," regularly prefixed in the former of the two—
"*That* man"—makes the meaning unmistakable. But this was
not the only meaning of the Aramaic phrase: its basic meaning *man* was still, of course, in constant use.

In approaching the thorny problem, What did Jesus mean
by the phrase—that is, did he use it as a title for himself?—
one further word of caution is necessary. Regardless of
whether Jesus did or did not identify himself with this supernatural figure, his followers eventually came to the belief
that he had. All three of the Synoptic Gospels accept this
view. Matthew and Luke are so sure of it that occasionally
they substitute the term "Son of man" for Mark's original
"I." Thus in the famous colloquy near Cæsarea Philippi,
instead of the Markan: "Who do man say that *I* am?" [6]
Matthew has edited it to stand: Who do man say that the
Son of man is?" [7]—while one form of the Matthæan text—
the so-called "Western text"—combines the two to read:
"Who do men say that *I, the Son of man,* am?" With this
may be compared Matthew's "Blessed are ye when men shall
reproach you, and persecute you, and say all manner of evil
against you falsely, *for my sake*" [8] and Luke's equivalent,
ending "for the Son of man's sake." [9] Naturally, editorial
alterations of this sort, and those cited are but two of several,

[6] Mark 8:27.   [7] Matt. 16:13.   [8] Matt. 5:11.
[9] Luke 6:22.

are to be disregarded as being evidence of Jesus' own usage.

In addition, there are at least two cases where the evidence of mistranslation is patent. In both cases "man," not "Son of man" is the only proper translation. This is a highly important point, for regularly these two passages have been cited as evidence of Jesus' peculiar "Messianic consciousness." One has to do with the Sabbath, the other with the forgiveness of sin. The one reads: "The sabbath was made for man, and not man for the sabbath: therefore. . . ." Actually the "therefore," as well as the whole nature of the section, suggests that "*man* is lord even of the sabbath" [10] is the only possible conclusion.

To see this word evidencing a claim on the part of Jesus to possess in his own right unique power over the Sabbath not only introduces a note not suggested by the context of the section and at variance with the emphasis in the other Sabbath passages, but also runs afoul of the clearly resultative force of the conjunctive, "so that" or "therefore." In addition, it deprives of its real insight a saying than which few profounder have ever been phrased: man is an end, not a means to some other end. He is ultimate, the touchstone of life. Every institution, every law, every form or product of government has permanence and value only in terms of its contribution to the life of man; as it makes for a fuller, richer, more complete life. Certainly, if this is the original meaning and can, without unwarranted wishful thinking, be with propriety ascribed to Jesus, it would go far toward answering our basic query, Why did this man make the impress which he did?

The other is equally clear. In answer to his critic's reproof of his effrontery in declaring the paralytic's sin forgiven,[11] for none save God could forgive sin, Jesus' word is explicit:

[10] Mark 2:27–28.   [11] Mark 2:1–12.

"That you may know that man does have authority to forgive sin . . . ." Certainly Matthew's conclusion to this incident, which he repeats: "But when the multitudes saw it, they were afraid, and glorified God, who had given such authority *unto men*," [12] is not to be overlooked.

But when both of these types of passages are removed— the one, editorial interpretation; the other, wrong translation: and both apparently reflecting the later view that this term had been Jesus' wonted substitute for "I"—there remain other passages where the term is patently an apocalyptic title. A fair example of these is the famous Markan word: "For whosoever shall be ashamed of *me* and of *my* words in this adulterous and sinful generation, the *Son of man* also shall be ashamed of him, when *he* cometh in the glory of *his* Father with the holy angels." [13]

It requires no argument that there is nothing in this passage to demand identification of the "me" and "my" with the "Son of man," "he," and "his" save the readers insistence that Jesus did use this queer paraphrase instead of "I–me," which is precisely the question under scrutiny.

If the position maintained through this book be accepted, that Jesus believed himself to be God's prophet, chosen and empowered to proclaim the dawn of the new age, the "kingdom of God," it requires very little "reading in" to see Jesus' use of "Son of man"—that is, "The Man"—in terms of the angelic supernatural figure whom God was speedily to send to inaugurate the Judgment and to preside over it.

Thus this passage would seem to mean: It is not failure to believe in Jesus or to adopt a right attitude toward him that is fatal. Rather it is the rejection of his message, which means not a rejection of the prophet, the herald, but of the One whose word he is proclaiming. Those who refuse to hearken

[12] Matt. 9:8.   [13] Mark 8:38.

to the herald's word are flouting, not the herald, but the King who sent him. This rejection is fatal and can only result in condemnation by the Son of man when he appears to sit upon his throne.

In this connection it is to be observed that while the evangelists were convinced that Jesus used the strange title to distinguish himself, they never allow another to use it as a title for Jesus. It is never "concerning him"; it appears only in his mouth. In the book of Acts—Volume II of the writing of which Luke is Volume I—the martyred Stephen cried out in his dying agony, "Behold, I see the heavens opened, and the Son of man standing on the right hand of God." [14] That this is of Lucan composition and intended as a strict fulfillment, deliberately reflecting the language of Jesus' prophetic word: "But from henceforth shall the Son of man be seated at the right hand of the power of God," [15] is highly probable and accounts for the exceptional usage.

Thus with regard to the term rendered "Son of man," five points would seem to be indicated:

1. That the phrase was on Jesus' lips constantly is highly probable.

2. That he meant himself thereby is far less certain, in fact most unlikely.

3. That his disciples eventually came to the belief that Jesus was and had claimed to be that figure, is likely.

4. That this identification was made after his death and not during his lifetime, is most naturally concluded from the evidence. That is, later "theological views" tended to obscure the more primitive note that as God's prophet Jesus had heralded the momentary advent of the supernatural "Son of man" and had felt himself to be his precursor.

5. The earlier use of the term by Jesus to indicate another,

[14] Acts 7:56.   [15] Luke 22:69.

not himself, resulted in a distinct modification of the message
of John the Baptist. In a word, the insistence in the Gospels
—so strangely absent from Josephus if historical [16]—that the
one function of John was to serve as the forerunner of his
greater successor is in essence an adaptation of Jesus' own
word that as God's prophet he was to prepare the way for
God's Final Judge, the heavenly Son of man, his own "greater
successor."

A further word of amplification of point 4 may be added.
In the postcrucifixion days the disciples' confident and passionate belief that Jesus, as God's prophet, had been under
the supernal blessing of God seemed to be challenged by his
shameful death on the cross—on Scriptural warrant proof
positive that he had been cursed, not blessed.[17] That during
those days they "saw" him is not likely to be questioned by
even the most determined antisupernaturalist. They "saw"
him in relation to the task to which his hold upon them was
driving them. It requires little historical imagination to recognize at the base of the rapidly developing "Christology" the
fundamental question: "Who then was he?" This was a question both insistent and natural to his intimates as they sought
to explain the grasp which the dead prophet still had upon
them.

That in the passage commonly styled "Peter's confession" [18]
is to be seen a reflection of this early postcrucifixion concern
would seem to me very probable. To be sure, Mark has transformed the "Who then *was* he" to "Who then am I," as a part

[16] Josephus, *Antt.* 18, 5, 2. In this brief, but seemingly unbiased or slanted,
statement, commonly accepted by scholars as genuine (unlike the "Christ
passage" [*Antt.* 18, 3, 3], which is patently a Christian interpolation into
Josephus' text), the absence from John's message of any reference to a
greater successor, of whom he (John) is but the prophetic voice, is adequately explained as being in accord with the facts, not a result of suppressing or altering them.

[17] Deut. 21:23.   [18] Mark 8:27–33.

of his theory of the Messianic secret which the Twelve, and they alone, were to grasp, and they but in only sorry part until the Resurrection. Actually, if Jesus claimed to be a prophet of God and was accepted as such, at least by his followers, such queries as "Who do men say . . ." or "Who do you say that I am?" are far from natural. Despite Mark—and his bequest to popular thought—there was no question at all as to this point.

But in the days of reconstruction it was of real moment. And it would seem most likely that it was the intriguing reference to the "Son of man" which brought the first advance in "seeing Jesus." This term had been constantly on his lips. Now that his restraining presence was gone, what more natural than to take the initial step to answer the question, "Who then was he?" Did not our hearts burn within us? And the answer? How blind have been our eyes, how obtuse our hearts! He was speaking of himself, and we thought he had meant another!

If this suggestion be accepted, we have before us the natural birth of the view, destined to bulk so large in subsequent thinking, of the "second coming," for by this identification Jesus' prediction of the speedy coming of the Son of man came to be seen as his promise of speedy and supernatural return. It was this belief which was the mainspring of the early postcrucifixion movement. It was this compulsion: so much to do, so little time; this obligation that when the Son of man returned he should find faith on the earth,[19] which drove them, as it was later to drive Saul of Tarsus, to the mission task.

And by this identification the new movement took its first step away from its parent Judaism. Many Jews shared the notion of the speedy end of the age. If they had not, Jesus

[19] Luke 18:8.

would never have dreamed that dream! The one distinguishing feature in this "new sect of Judaism" was their confident claim: "And it is by the return of our crucified leader that this end of the age will take place." [20]

A generation ago many volumes were produced attempting to diagnose Jesus' psychic health and regularly arriving at conclusions which, while generally at variance one with another, had the common result of scandalizing orthodox Christians. Few of the authors were historians with competence in the essential problem of sources. Regularly they used all four of the gospels indifferently and as if they were clinical charts produced by on-the-spot, trained observers. In consequence, their conclusions were at best highly speculative, not infrequently grotesque. Yet the rash diagnoses of such alienists as William Hirsch and Binet-Sanglé [21] are but the logical outcome of the orthodox insistence upon Jesus' "messianic self-consciousness," especially in terms of his acceptance of the rôle and title Son of man.

Schweitzer, who was insisting in his view of "thoroughgoing eschatology" that Jesus had seen himself in the cosmic rôle of the supernatural Son of man speedily to come, and that he had flung himself on the wheel in a vain attempt to make it turn, incurred the charge by many of his New Testament colleagues, notably Adolf Jülicher, of ascribing to Jesus "an insane conceit which no eschatological enthusiasm ex-

[20] Those who wish to examine these contentions in more detail are referred to my *Christian Beginnings*, esp. pp. 170 f.; to an article "The Date of Peter's Confession" in *Quantulacumque—Studies Presented to Kirsopp Lake* by *Pupils, Colleagues, and Friends* (London: Christophers, 1937), pp. 117–122; and to "And That He Hath Been Raised" in *Jewish Quarterly Review*, XLIII, No. 1 (July, 1952), pp. 27–56.

[21] A penetrating examination and appraisal of the views of several of these writers is to be found in Walter E. Bundy's *The Psychic Health of Jesus*.

cuses." When Schweitzer determined to leave academic circles for life as a mission doctor, his medical thesis was devoted to a criticism of the uncritical pathographic literature about Jesus. What was properly to be seen as an "eschatological fixed idea" was, Schweitzer maintained, far removed from ecstasy, epilepsy, or paranoia, which the several writers had so recklessly argued were to be discerned.[22]

Many of Schweitzer's arguments—especially his thoroughgoing attack upon this juvenile use of critically unsound materials—were warranted and sound. There is a vast gulf between the thought world of the first century and the twentieth. Men of sobriety did hold views then which, were they to be endorsed today, would insure their activities of suspicion if not of restraint. But there are nonetheless limits which the historian must face, even though he makes use of the ancient word in a defensible, if not original, sense: "Your thoughts are not my thoughts."

For a man in the first century in Palestine to believe in the near approach of the end of the world and to envisage the presence of a supernatural angelic, nonhuman figure at its consummation is entirely possible; but for him to toy with the idea that he—a flesh-and-blood human being—either was or would be transformed into such a character is quite another matter. If the evidence forced the critic to see that Jesus had so believed, he would have to accept the conclusions. At the same time it is hard to see how he could escape the corollary of assuming a departure from normalcy so wide as to require a pathographic conclusion.

But such evidence does not exist. Recognition that this identification of Jesus was not made by the man himself but

---

[22] *Die psychiatrische Beurteilung Jesu.* This 46-page book was finally translated into English in 1948 under the title, *The Psychiatric Study of Jesus.*

by his followers changes the whole problem. After his death his disciples might well come to the conclusion that they had erred in thinking his constant reference to the coming "Son of man" was a prediction of the advent of another. Instead, they were now sure, he had meant himself. With their confidence—they lived in the first century, not the twentieth—that he was now with God in heaven (as were Enoch and Elijah certainly, Moses in all likelihood), why might he not return at any moment on the clouds?

In consequence, I find it hard to understand the pain of many orthodox Christians (to whom this whole matter of ancient speculation—end of the world, supernatural visitations, and consequent final judgment—must be at most far removed) at the thought that Jesus' hypothetical self-identification, which can be explained only as due to a more then serious mental disturbance, is not demanded by the evidence or even, in the judgment of many cautious students, probable.

That Jesus of Nazareth, as every other man who has been seized by the overpowering conviction that he has been chosen by God for a specific task and filled with his spirit to such a degree that when he speaks it is not he but God who speaks, was what is often styled "an emotionally excitable man" would seem highly probable. At times he may have seemed "beside himself" and thus, to his contemporaries, possessed by a spirit not his own; at other times he very likely bore evidence of the soberest discretion and could bring at least momentary quiet to others in the clutches of powers not their own. Surely it is often the presence of contradictory and conflicting elements—many facets to the one stone—which makes a personality attractive, amazing, and compelling. At our remove, attempts to be more precise are impossible. It would nonetheless seem unwarranted to close

our eyes to occasional flashes which illumine the distant
scene, even though we are unable to explain with scientific
nicety the precise cause of the light.

One final postscript may be added. Whether all students
of these now far-distant days accept these conclusions, which
are offered with far less certainty than their, at times necessarily brief and highly simplified, statement might imply, one
detail would seem certain. The term "Son of man," whether
Jesus did or did not employ it for himself, indicated a supernatural figure of cosmic importance, an angel far removed
from common clay, and quite apart from "flesh and blood."
Thus for preachers to persist in using the term as an antith-
esis to "Son of God": "He was both 'Son of God' and 'Son
of man,'" is unqualifiedly wrong and misleading. The term
did not connote participation in the common lot of men,
either by humble birth or amazing condescension. It was a
unique and—to adopt a modern phrase—an "altogether
other" figure. There were many "sons of God"; there was,
could be, but *one* "Son of man."

15

"What mean such mighty works wrought by his hands?"

Through the years there have been few problems more consequential to readers of the Christian story than that of the miracles which it is recorded Jesus wrought. In the early years they constituted no problem at all. Not only he but his followers—not alone his immediate disciples but those centuries later—performed them as a matter of course. In more recent years, with a radically different outlook on life, in which notions of an orderly universe have come more and more to the fore, there has been a marked reduction of the area in which such stories are to be accepted as historically certain or even probable. Such stories, ascribed to later worthies and once regarded as a proof of their sainthood, came to be dismissed as folklore, legend, or even worse. But despite the limitation of the field in which miracles were deemed possible, there was an even surer confidence that for Jesus and his immediate followers they were certain. In a word, canonicity insured historicity. Stories recorded in the gospels and the book of Acts were divinely attested and guaranteed; those of precisely the same nature, if recorded

149

elsewhere of other folk, were to be dismissed as fairy tales, to be believed only by the credulous, held in the sway of an ecclesiastical hierarchy. But the same stories in the gospels were totally different. They were the guarantees of Jesus' unique nature; to deny them was to reject him. And there are many who still share that view.

To others the situation is a bit more complicated. A growing knowledge of the seemingly well-attested laws to which our world seems in tune has raised problems. Nature miracles, in which manifest violations of the processes and procedures of life as we know them seem involved, have become increasingly soft-pedaled. Again and again we are offered as brand-new insights of their champions old arguments and "common-sense" explanations, which the now almost forgotten seventeenth- and eighteenth-century rationalists, notably Dr. Paulus,[1] had advanced, only to see them mercilessly demolished by such critics as David Friedrich Strauss[2] and Bruno Bauer. One is reminded of the old saying: "Anyone can be original if he is ignorant enough!"

A bit awkward, those nature miracles—levitation upon water, the transformation of water into wine, multiplying

[1] H. E. G. Paulus (1761–1851), for forty years a professor at Heidelberg, was the most meticulously thoroughgoing of all the rationalists in seeking to disengage, as he phrased it, fact from opinion: the evangelists thought they were recording miracles; actually they were insufficiently acquainted with the laws of nature to understand the secondary causes. His two-volume *Leben Jesu* (never translated into English) has as its full title: *"The Life of Jesus as the Basis of a Purely Historical Account of Early Christianity."* Paulus was a deeply religious man and most appreciative of Jesus. The miracles were not historically true, to be sure, but the stories recounting them were not due to fraud, as Reimarus and the Deists had insisted. Rather they were the result of innocent misunderstanding on the part of naïve observers.

[2] Strauss' first Life of Jesus—*Das Leben Jesu* (1835), translated into English by none less than George Eliot—stands as one of the great landmarks in what has been styled "the quest of the historical Jesus." Many of Strauss' pronouncements would need to be restated in the light of the re-

a tiny bit of food into a prodigious amount, finding a silver coin in the mouth of a fish, staying a windstorm and surging sea by a word of command, blasting a fig tree because it did not carry fruit at a season when it could not reasonably be expected so to do. To get around the problem without flatly denying the miracles—that would have been irreverent— they were judiciously explained away.

With regard to the "healing miracles," fresh courage was taken. The findings of the psychiatrists, with their confident plumbing of the recesses of the human mind and their predilection for the abnormal and pathological (and how much of it they are finding!), plus the discoveries in what is now commonly referred to as "psychosomatic" medicine, have provided a most attractive way out of an embarrassing dilemma. Here was to be found *bona fide,* scientifically veri- fied proof of the historical accuracy of the reports of Jesus' healing ministry. In consequence, while there is no report of claims by nonecclesiastically-trained meteorologists that their attempts at changes of weather—by seeding clouds or discouraging hurricanes— are a vindication of any of the gospel stories, we do have enthusiastic reports of faith- healing clinics, no longer restricted to the more tangential groups, but operated by college- and seminary-trained ex- perts most ecclesiastically correct. And their cures, they are sure, are but verifications of Jesus.

Despite the excesses and overemphasis, which are hon- estly admitted by the experts in their study of the human mind and its many quirks, there have been profound and revolutionary discoveries and advances made in these several

---

search since his day, but his tremendous contribution, although weakened by his overconfidence that his key would open all locks—an overconfidence, alas, shared by many lesser successors—might with profit be studied afresh today.

fields. But that this in the slightest degree affects our understanding of the stories in the gospels is a totally different matter. Proficiency in these newer sciences has been the result of years of the most demanding research and study. To read them back into a Palestinian peasant of the first century would seem but the latest of many similar attempts to make the one they are attempting to defend against modern doubts over into their own image. Or again, to change the figure, they are but fresh refusals to permit a first-century Jew to think and believe and act as a first-century Jew. To the historian such attempts are both awkward and unconvincing.

That back of the several stories of the exorcism of evil spirits lies a core of sober fact, would appear to me entirely probable, as has already been suggested in an earlier chapter. Nor is it at all impossible that behind such a story as that of the cure of the woman with the chronic hemorrhage,[3] is to be seen an actual fact. There may very well have been a drastic, if momentary, effect in passionate belief that the one to whom she appealed had the divine power to heal her. And certainly if, as has been constantly urged in these pages, Jesus believed himself to be and was believed by many of his hearers to be possessed by the spirit of God, her confidence would seem justified. What makes these, and the myriad other, ancient stories of the effect for good and ill of the blessing or curse seem to us so remote is our lack of belief in their compelling efficiency. Granted the belief that the word was freighted with power, there is little ground for wonder that on occasion the effect was realized.[4] To a modern Ananias the dread word of a modern Peter would likely be no more than an empty gesture—the equivalent

[3] Mark 5:25–34; cf. Matt. 9:20–22 and Luke 8:43–48.
[4] Cf. Acts 5:1–11; I Cor. 5:1–5.

of the modern "go to hell," which is at best but a noncompelling vulgarism. But to an emotionally distraught man who believed that such a curse could be effective, it might well so prove.

Nor is it to be overlooked that in several of the stories, both of exorcism and of healing, there remain traces surprisingly like those encountered in accounts of the activities of the professional thaumaturge: not only the use of spittle and clay,[5] but more specifically the sudden and unexplained burst of anger which is unmistakable in the technical word employed in several of the stories,[6] and which has so perplexed and embarrassed both translators and interpreters. These suggest the possibility that underlying the accounts as they now stand in the gospels may well have been a tradition suggesting a more primitive technique. It is scarcely accidental that in the later versions of the Markan story of the cleansing of the leper,[7] this strange "snort of anger"—more natural to the exorcist than to the figure whose word is instantly effective, even at a distance from the sufferer [8]—is quietly omitted.

In the ancient world there were many cases of the hasty burial of an apparently dead person, who, as a subsequent opening of the grave revealed, had awakened from his coma to a living death. It has been conjectured that underlying our gospel stories in which Jesus raised the dead there may well have been this simpler explanation.

A far more probable source for the stories in which Jesus

[5] Cf. Mark 8:22–26; John 9:6 ff.

[6] ἐμβριμησάμενος (Mark 1:43); ἐνεβριμήσατο (John 11:33); ἐμβριμώμενος (John 11:38); ἐνεβριμήθη (Matt. 9:30). For a very rewarding study of the ancient techniques of exorcism, see C. Bonner, "Traces of Thaumaturgic Technique in the Miracles," in *Harvard Theological Review*, XX, No. 3 (July, 1927), pp. 171–181.

[7] Matt. 8:1–4; Luke 5:12–16.

[8] Cf. Matt. 8:5–13 and Luke 7:1–10; cf. John 4:46–54.

restored the dead is to be found in the similar tales long told
of Elijah [9] and Elisha.[10] It is not surprising that the followers
of Jesus very speedily and naturally came to see predictions
of him—his words and deeds—in the all-inclusive Scriptures.
They were convinced that they were the true Judaism. God's
promises and blessings were theirs; naturally in the blueprint
for the future which God had revealed to the world centuries
before, this all-important chapter was to be found. And they
speedily found it!

Evidence of this confidence is to be found everywhere, and
has already been mentioned in passing. One of the number-
less examples may suffice: "These are my words which I
spake unto you, while I was yet with you, that all things must
needs be fulfilled, *which are written in the law of Moses, and
the prophets, and the psalms, concerning me.*" [11] Nor is this
to be seen as any long-delayed Christian discovery. To Paul
it is a confidence that needed no argument. Again, but one
of many evidences of this conviction must suffice: "For I
delivered unto you first of all that which also I received:
that Christ died for our sins *according to the Scriptures;*
and that he was buried; and that he hath been raised on the
third day *according to the Scriptures....*" [12] The fact that
has so perplexed many students, the long delay in the appearance of the gospels, recounting the all-important events
of the crucified leader, is after all not so surprising. Together
with the persistent conviction—Jesus' abiding heritage to his
followers—of the momentary end of the age, which made
pointless preserving a chronicle for a later age which would
never be born, was the certainty that it all stood recorded
in Holy Writ, open to all who had eyes to see.[13]

[9] I Kings 17:17–24.   [10] II Kings 4:32–37.   [11] Luke 24:44.
[12] I Cor. 15:3 f.
[13] A few hours spent in reading the second-century Justin Martyr, for
example, will probably convince any reader that this statement is factual.

There was no formal moment when this notion was devised or even regarded as something new. To men who for centuries had been convinced of the fundamental nature of these all-precious revelations, whatever arose was automatically believed to have been foreseen and predicted. Thus, as soon as Jesus was regarded by his hearers as a prophet sent to them by God, written evidences of him were ready to hand, with crystal-clear indication of what he was to do: "And in that day shall the deaf hear the words of the book, and the eyes of the blind shall see out of obscurity and out of darkness." [14] "Then the eyes of the blind shall be opened, and the ears of the deaf shall be unstopped. Then shall the lame man leap as a hart, and the tongue of the dumb shall sing . . . ." [15] These, and they are but two of many, must be fulfilled. This was "that day." It is not necessary to assume that a formal catena of such passages had been ordered by Judaism against the coming of an expected one, as earlier scholars occasionally postulated. Instead, when a figure appeared who was able to convince his hearers of his divine commission and heaven-sent message, there was a wealth of material from which there speedily began to be formed stories of what he was doing and saying.

It is quite unnecessary to toy with the notion that one day, as he had talked to a multitude of listeners, his generous act in sharing his own luncheon had encouraged others to like generosity, with the result that all had eaten; and later, that a miraculous element was added to a simple story. Thus the numerous tasteless attempts to rationalize the stories, to remove the later miraculous intrusions by a sort of spiritual fractional distillation and thereby to recover the original,

---

Predictions of Jesus—the so-called "Messianic prophecies"—abound and were found in the most unlikely places.

[14] Isa. 29:18.   [15] Isa. 35:5 f.

are wrongly slanted and misleading. The miraculous element
is not a later and unfortunate addition; on the contrary, it
is the one basic element in the story, the cause of the story
being told. In this case, the story of Elisha feeding the hundred men with twenty loaves of barley and fresh ears of
grain, of which "they did eat, and left thereof," [16] is surely
a much more natural basis for the story of the two miraculous
feedings performed by Elisha's far greater successor, than
are the labored attempts of the rationalists to save a far
from impressive "historical nucleus."

Similarly, attempts to see a natural explanation underlying
the stilling of the storm on the Sea of Galilee [17]—suddenly
the boat rounded a promontory and was shielded from the
disastrous gust—are definitely pedestrian. More difficult of
explanation than the sudden staying of wind and wave would
be the antics of the folk in the boat, several of whom pre-
sumably were experienced fishermen. Their amazement at
what would seem a far from unusual experience on a valley-
skirted lake is surpassed by their standing up and moving
around in the boat. Similarly Jesus' ability, not to stay the
wind, but to stand up in a tossing boat, is a feat not to be
minimized. In a word, the story, as it now stands, seems
far from a first-hand account from folks accustomed to fish-
ing trips on Galilee's lake, and attempts to account "ration-
ally" for certain details in a story where all the other details
are equally perplexing would seem a thankless task. Nor is
it at all necessary. A far more ready-to-hand explanation of
the story is to be found in the numerous poetic accounts of
the Lord's prowess in this particular sort of act. Psalm
107:23–30—

[16] II Kings 4:42–44.
[17] Mark 4:35–41; cf. Matt. 8:23–27 and Luke 8:22–25.

They that go down to the sea in ships,
That do business in great waters;
These see the works of the LORD,
And his wonders in the deep.
For he commandeth, and raiseth the stormy wind,
Which lifteth up the waves thereof.
They mount up to the heavens,
   they go down again to the depths:
Their soul melteth away because of trouble.
They reel to and fro, and stagger like a drunken man.
And are at their wits' end.
Then they cry unto the LORD in their trouble,
And he bringeth them out of their distresses.
He maketh the storm a calm,
So that the waves thereof are still.
Then are they glad because they are quiet;
So he bringeth them unto their desired haven—

and 89:9—

Thou rulest the pride of the sea:
When the waves thereof arise, thou stillest them—

would certainly seem a most likely source of the story. These
are but two of many references to this so-popular theme.[18]

It would be a thankless and absurd task to attempt to date
the emergence of this miracle story and that—this one took
its present form during Jesus' ministry; that one three years
later. The whole point is, with the wealth of material contained in the Old Testament there would seem little or nothing to prevent a constant finding of him in these pages from
the first moment he had impressed his hearers with his cre-
dentials. The real and perpetual miracle is thus not the
stories told about him but the impress which he made upon
his hearers, which led them to accept him as a prophet sent

[18] Cf. Psalms 29:3; 46:3; 93:3 f., Nah. 1:4; II Macc. 9:8.

of God and to persist in that conviction despite the hostility
and seeming triumph of his foes. Grant him this achievement
—and to deny it is to leave the whole story without any
rational explanation, save the hypothesis of a *deus ex machina*
which surpasses anything even Euripides could devise—and
the story is understandable. More than that, there comes
into proper focus as the real explanation the power of the
man himself, quite without the appeal to supernatural intervention, whose only evidence is stubborn faith, or to the re-
writing of ancient stories in such a way as to remove all
which the ancient world saw of significance in them in order
to leave room for the intrusion of what seems to us prosily
natural.

Explanations which are harder to credit than the difficulties which they seek to explain are to most academic dis-
ciplines suspect, even if to the theologian they are attractive
and convincing.

16

"Go not into any way of the gentiles"

ALL THREE of the Synoptic gospels represent Jesus selecting a group of twelve men whom he on occasion sent out on preaching missions akin to his own and with whom he became increasingly intimate and confidential. That several of these named intimates were at an early date prominent in the constantly increasing number of followers of the crucified prophet is adequately attested by references to them in the letters of Paul. On the other hand, the precise number twelve, so obvious a reflection of the traditional "twelve tribes," together with the uncertainty as to several of the "twelve"—for the lists show surprising minor variations [1]—suggests that our accounts reflect an outlook after

[1] Four lists of the Twelve occur: Mark 3:16–19; Matt. 10:2–4; Luke 6:14–16; Acts 1:13. In addition to slight variations of order in these lists there are at least seeming differences. A "Simon" (other than Peter) occurs in all four lists, but in Mark and Matthew he is styled "the Cananæan," in Luke and Acts "the Zealot." Mark (certainly) and Matthew (probably) have "Thaddæus," although in some manuscripts "Lebbæus" or "Lebbæus called Thaddæus" is to be found. In Luke and Acts, instead of "Thaddæus/ Lebbæus" there is listed a "Judas of James." In the Gospel of John the

Jesus' death, when study of the Scriptures for additional support of the growing movement had resulted in a greater emphasis upon the twelve tribes than would seem natural for an itinerant prophet in a land where the actuality of twelve tribes was at best but a hazy memory.

At this remove precise details in such matters are scarcely to be expected, but some points would seem reasonably certain. That among the many who were eager in their acceptance of Jesus' proclamation were some who became increasingly intimate and became, so to speak, full-time followers, would certainly seem a cautious conclusion. Nor is it unlikely that the word which now stands in the Matthæan version of Jesus' instructions to them, "Go not into any way of the Gentiles, and enter not into any city of the Samaritans: but go rather to the lost sheep of the house of Israel" [2]—quite apart from the likelihood that the story as we now have it [3] reflects a much later day, when Christian missionaries were going out two by two and needed precise instructions as to proper procedure—reflects the outlook, if not the precise phraseology, of Jesus himself.

The absence of any echo of protest by Jesus' enemies, eager to find ammunition against him, is not to be overlooked. Nor should we forget the conservative attitude of the early disciples, evident in their suspicious hostility to Paul and so revealing in the primitive-sounding story of the vision from heaven which Peter required as a prelude to his contact with the gentile Cornelius.[4] Had Jesus championed or evidenced a point of view where Jew and gentile stood alike, it is

---

term, "the Twelve," occurs four times, but no formal list of names is given. Of the twelve names listed in the Synoptic gospels specific mention by name in John is restricted to Peter, Andrew, Philip, Thomas, and Judas Iscariot, who is three times styled "Judas of *Simon* Iscariot."

[2] Matt. 10:5 f.   [3] Matt, 10:1–11:1.
[4] Acts 10:1–48, (esp. 9–23).

extraordinarily difficult to understand how his followers could have proved so obtuse. Nor is the story of the grudging healing of the daughter of the foreign woman[5] to be forgotten, with the revealing word: "Let the children first be filled: for it is not meet to take the children's bread and cast it to the dogs." Attempts to explain away the seemingly brutal word, which evidences the century-long confidence of being the "chosen people," as a gentle test by Jesus, and with an imagined tender smile playing over his face, are far from impressive. Instead the impression is clear that in this respect Jesus was a completely orthodox Jew, to whom the gentiles were naturally, but without especial concern, viewed as "dogs" and "swine."[6]

Long before our gospels took their present shape the gentile mission had become definitely established. This had not happened overnight; but through the years missionaries, of whom Paul is a notable but far from solitary example, had found a much more favorable audience for their message among the once-despised gentiles. In consequence, this circumstance too was discovered to be predicted and blessed in the all-encompassing pages of Scripture. God never changes. Since he was now so manifestly blessing the movement, he had always so intended. More than that, Jesus, who was now believed to have shared God's counsels from the beginning, had of course thus intended.

Explanations of the precise details varied. The basic confidence was sure. In the Gospel of Matthew the thesis is clear. During his ministry Jesus had restricted himself solely to the Jews. Thus none of them might with propriety protest that the now almost completely gentile movement had arisen

---

[5] Mark 7:24–30 and Matt. 15:21–28—a story which Luke conveniently omits.

[6] Cf. Matt. 7:6, another verse absent in Luke.

in consequence of his wanton neglect of the chosen people. Instead, it was their rejection of the one sent to them that had resulted in the rightabout-face of the Great Commission: "Go ye therefore, and make disciples of all the nations." [7]

Luke's explanation was far different. From the very beginning Jesus had envisaged the gentile mission, as was proved by his reference to the activities of Elijah and Elisha in the account of the rejection at Nazareth [8]—a Markan story not only amplified by Luke, but moved forward to serve as the first peal of what was to prove increasingly the basic melodic note. Thus in Luke we find the stories of Jesus and Samaritans: the entrance into the Samaritan village (a seemingly deliberate correction of Matthew's direct prohibition) [9]; the parable of the Good Samaritan [10]; the grateful Samaritan leper. [11] Indeed it is not too much to say that the long section in Luke (9:51–18:14), which is inserted into the Markan outline at the precise moment when Jesus is to leave Galilee for Jerusalem, is intended by Luke as a deliberate parallel to the preceding ministry in Galilee. The one had been to the Jews; this one, in which Samaritans are to the fore, was a foretaste of the coming gospel mission. [12] Nor is it to be overlooked that it is in this section that there occurs the story of the sending out of the Seventy [13]—an undeniable Lucan doublet of the story of the sending out of

---

[7] Matt. 28:19.   [8] Luke 4:16–30.

[9] Luke 9:51–56. Contrast Matt. 10:5.   [10] Luke 10:30–37.

[11] Luke 17:11–19, a story which is heavily dependent upon the earlier Markan story (Mark 1:40–45; Matt. 8:1–4; Luke 5:12–16) and with its emphasis upon the proper attitude shown by the Samaritan in contrast to that of the Jews—a point similarly stressed in the story of the Good Samaritan—anticipating the coming mission to the gentiles, who would prove receptive as the Jews had not.

[12] As soon as this is recognized, the appropriateness of the story of the initial rejection in a *Samaritan* village—a palpable doublet to the story of the initial rejection in Galilee—is evident.

[13] Luke 10:1–20.

the Twelve. Seventy was the traditional number of the gentile
nations. That the one story is the deliberate foil and balance
to the other, and has no historical basis in fact, would seem
certain.

This by no means is intended to imply that Jesus' attitude
was deliberately or markedly antigentile. In all probability
for him the matter was one of no more especial concern than
it was for any other Jew. Attempts to see him as a reformer
in the matter of race relations are as thankless and unwarranted as are all attempts to make him at home in the modern
world and, more specifically, the justification, if not the
sponsor, of our concern for social betterment. To the one
convinced that the bell had already sounded, matters such
as these paled into insignificance. In the Age to Come,
speedily to dawn, abuses and evils would be corrected; but
there seems little reason to assume that in his eyes the supe-
riority of a people which God himself had announced was
an abuse needing reform.

Attempts to see in Jesus a separatist, who had broken
away from Judaism and was intent upon founding a new
religion in which all men stood alike in the eyes of God, with
all "middle walls of partition" broken down, are simply
grotesque, despite their good intentions. If anything is certain, it is that in the early months—in all probability, the
early years—after the crucifixion the band of followers whom
he had impressed and quickened remained, as had he, loyal
and orthodox Jews, even though they had quickly come to
see the crucified prophet as the heaven-sent agent of God,
who would speedily return to establish the kingdom which
he had announced and for which he had died.

In all other respects they seem to have remained devout
Jews. The opposition which they encountered, and which

gradually made further fields seems fairer, would appear to have been aroused by the dangerous nature of their message —the impending end of the age—which they sounded forth as had their leader before them.

In several of the early stories there are clear, if unobtrusive, touches, indicating no desire or thought on the part of the early disciples to forsake the Judaism which had mothered them. It was not until the "sabbath was past" [14] that the women are reported as seeking Jesus' tomb. Peter and John "were going up into the temple at the hour of prayer, being the ninth hour." [15] And we must not forget the early reluctance to have contact with gentiles, particularly clear in such a story as Peter's experience in Joppa,[16] and the rigid insistence on such requirements as circumcision and the observance of dietary niceties, which led to a grave suspicion of Paul.[17]

Words and acts which are ascribed to Jesus and which stand in marked contrast to the outlook and practice of the days when our gospels appeared are their own best guarantee. The normal tendency was to see Jesus in perfect harmony with what his later followers had come to accept as God's changeless intent. In consequence, words attributed to him, evidencing a point of view contrary to that current at the later date, have the *prima facie* right to be regarded primitive tradition which has been preserved, not a later view read back. It was on this essentially sound premise that Schmiedel listed his famed nine pillar passages, which he insisted must be genuine because it was inconceivable that later Christians could have invented them.[18]

---

[14] Mark 16:1.   [15] Acts 3:1.   [16] Acts 10:1–48.
[17] Cf. Acts 15:1–29; Gal. 2:11 ff.
[18] P. W. Schmiedel, article "Gospels," in *Encyclopædia Biblica*, II, col. 1881. This book-length article has by no means lost its value for the modern serious student.

Thus the not infrequent citation of two passages in Matthew, in which the word "church" appears in words ascribed to Jesus, and the persistent claim that they evidence his basic aim, namely, the establishment of a (Christian) church in separation from the Jewish synagogue, are definitely unwarranted. The word *church* occurs but twice in the whole gospel tradition, and both times in passages which are commonly and properly regarded as comparatively late and improbable as genuine words of Jesus. The one, "Thou art Peter, and upon this rock I will build my church," [19] is surely a late addition to the earlier account given in Mark. In the Markan story Peter is the recipient of a rebuke by Jesus in connection with his famous confession.[20] The Matthæan addition of Jesus' blessing of Peter—which certainly is to be seen as arising in what may be safely styled a "Petrine centre," not improbably Antioch, and not inconceivably in deliberate opposition to the later claims of Jerusalem for pre-eminence because their leader was James, the brother of Jesus—can hardly be understood save as the attempt by the later evangelist to guard his reader from the notion suggested by the terser Markan account that Jesus had disapproved Peter's acclamation.

The other passage,[21] where the church is mentioned in connection with directions for the conduct of members, one with another, must be understood as a page of practice from an early church manual and as coming from a time decades later than the prophet, who was calling his hearers to preparation for a new day, not to a code of procedure, in an organization eventually to be established in an unending world.

The failure of the Day to dawn, a day which he had so confidently believed, up to the very last, that he would see with his own eyes—that for the prophet, who had so surely

---

[19] Matt. 16:18.   [20] Mark 8:27–33.   [21] Matt. 18:17.

"known he was right," must indeed have been the terrible tragedy and disillusion. Small wonder the cry of agony: "My God, my God, why hast thou forsaken me?"! It is surely very shortsighted to seek to turn this so-honest agony into scarcely explainable—or justifiable—play-acting, as it would have been had Jesus known of the speedy triumph that was to be his "after three days," and of the steady growth of what was destined to "overcome the world." It was surely not the physical pain of the nails but the utter failure of his mission and his God, in the collapse of all that had seemed so certain and divinely sure—for the promised Day had not dawned!— that elicited the terrible cry, "My God, my God, Why?"

17

"He stedfastly set his face to go to Jerusalem"

APPARENTLY MOST of the seemingly brief prophetic activity of Jesus was in Galilee. Such is the picture presented in the Gospel of Mark and repeated in Matthew and Luke. The very different picture presented in John, with an essentially Judea-centred ministry, interrupted by brief trips to Galilee, from which he was constantly returning to Jerusalem to attend this feast or another, generally Passovers, has seemed to most students quite improbable. But it must be frankly faced that the Markan arrangement is apparently the product of that evangelist's own ingenuity in arranging and articulating a collection of short and undated sayings and doings in such a way as to make vivid his theory of the Messianic secret, which did not come to be fully known, even to the closest followers, until in the light of the Resurrection.

If this be granted, the Markan sketch, which for the past seventy-five years has been commonly accepted as the certain outline to be followed, must be viewed as based on theology rather than history. The fact that both Matthew and Luke follow this outline is simply unmistakable evidence that they both knew and adopted the earlier book as a source. Their repetition would in no wise add to the historical nature of the source they were employing unless they had independent and confirming knowledge—and for this there is no slightest evidence. Thus the commonly styled "threefold witness" is actually not such. Mark and Mark alone is our solitary guide.

That it was in Jerusalem that Jesus met his death is properly regarded by all historians as an assured fact, unlike most of the other details of the story—the several incidents and their sequence. Accordingly, if Mark is correct in his overall picture of an itinerant ministry in Galilee, regardless of its length or order of events, Jesus must have left Antipas' territory for a trip to Jerusalem at some time prior to the tragic end. How long before, however, like all other details of his ministry, is far from certain. Very probably the time in Jerusalem was brief, although the traditional scant six days, beginning with the "Hail, hail" of the crowds on Sunday and ending with the tragic and disillusioned "My God, my God" on the following Friday, is hardly to be pressed as chronologically exact. An amazing amount seems to be compressed in the record of those final days of tragedy. Furthermore, a somewhat longer story would seem to be suggested by the traditional lament, "O Jerusalem, Jerusalem, that killeth the prophets, and stoneth them that are sent unto her! *how often* would I have gathered thy children together . . ." which Matthew [1] sets early in those days, and which Luke, with rather less appropriateness, seemingly records as uttered while Jesus was still in Galilee.[2]

[1] Matt. 23:37–39.
[2] Luke 13:34–35. Or perhaps during the geographically uncertain "gentile ministry," parallel to the Jewish ministry in Galilee (*see* preceding chapter). Apparently Luke conceives the trip south through Samaria (not through

But the brevity of the period in Zion would seem highly probable, not because of the later traditional and conventionalized picture in what is commonly styled the "passion narrative," but because of the nature of Jesus' message and the potential dangers of riots and stern reprisals by Rome, which the authorities not unnaturally dreaded and sought to forestall.

Occasional narratives, which now stand during the days in Galilee, show Jesus making unexplained trips outside Galilee—once toward the coast of the Mediterranean to the "borders of Tyre and Sidon"; [3] at another time to Cæsarea Philippi,[4] the capital city of Philip the tetrarch and thus outside Antipas' domain. It is surely far from improbable that these trips were inspired by the desire to elude the police of Galilee's governor, Herod Antipas, who may well have become increasingly concerned at the potential danger to be seen in the effect the wandering prophet was having on many of the populace. Indeed, the paragraphs in Josephus, plausibly explaining the cause of the arrest and execution of John the Baptist, may well be pondered in the case of Jesus, too:

Now, when many others came in crowds about him, for they were greatly moved by hearing his words, Herod, who feared lest the great influence John had over the people might put it into his power and inclination to raise a rebellion (for they seemed

---

the Perea) but at the same time *via* Jericho. The seeming explanation of this very unlikely travel itinerary is twofold: it would set the proleptic "gentile" (Samaritan) ministry in Samaria; it evidences a knowledge of Palestinian geography far from profound, for apparently he thought Jericho somewhere in Samaria. Otherwise the intimation in the story of the Good Samaritan that the latter not infrequently made the trip from Jerusalem to Jericho would be at best surprising (Luke 10:35).

[3] Mark 7:24 ff.

[4] Mark 8:27; Matt. 16:13. Luke follows Mark in recording the incident (9:18), but without mention of the place name.

ready to do anything he should advise), thought it best, by putting him to death, to prevent any mischief he might cause, and not bring himself into difficulties, by sparing a man who might make him repent of it when it should be too late.[5]

With the adoption of the traditional picture of Jesus abandoned by all save the Twelve, to whom he devoted himself almost exclusively during the final months, this menace in the eyes of the local tetrarch has been commonly overlooked. But if, as has been suggested in an earlier chapter, there seems little warrant for the popular notion of a waning enthusiasm in Galilee, but rather a probability that when Jesus went to Jerusalem he left a highly enthusiastic and devoted following behind, there may well have been frequent times when it had seemed wise to absent himself from such centres as Capernaum and Tiberias for regions less immediately under the eye of Antipas. That acute and able governor, who had remained secure in the saddle for well over thirty years, had the reputation of standing high in the favor of Tiberius in Rome, both because of his success in keeping his own territory free from uprisings and disorder, and because of his zeal in keeping that always-suspicious emperor informed of any potential danger or unrest in the East.[6]

Much has been conjectured as to what led Jesus to make the fateful trip to Jerusalem. That his work had collapsed in Galilee and that accordingly he was seeking new and fairer fields may be dismissed as unlikely. Nonetheless, it is far from impossible that, despite the growing and enthusiastic crowds that dogged his steps, Jesus was becoming disturbed. The end had not yet come. The kingdom had not dawned. Was there growing in his mind a conviction that

[5] Josephus, *Antt.* 18, 5, 2.

[6] In consequence, Antipas was far from popular among his fellow governors, as is suggested in Luke's mention of the "former enmity" with Pontius Pilate (Luke 23:12).

God was holding back the day until all had heard, notably in "Zion, whither the tribes go up"? When he stood in Jerusalem and uttered his cry—as Amos before him had done in Bethel and Samaria—the moment might well come and the wheel start to turn.

It is easy to exaggerate in what is at best conjecture. In part due to Luke's word, "for it cannot be that a prophet perish out of Jerusalem," [7] it has often been conjectured that Jesus set out for the city to the south with the express purpose and certainty that he would there be put to death. Schweitzer, to cite but one influential champion of this view, climaxed his moving picture of the imperious prophet of the new day as determined to inaugurate it by forcing the wheel to turn through flinging himself upon it.

And there is good seeming support for this view in the gospel stories. Mark, followed by both Matthew and Luke, represents Jesus—after the dawning insight of the Twelve near Cæsarea Philippi—as constantly talking about his coming death and resurrection. Three times [8] he expands that theme in seemingly so clear and exact a wise that none can fail to understand his meaning. And even God himself had confirmed it, six days after the first enunciation: "Hear ye him," [9] that is, believe (as Peter did not!) his word of the necessity for his death at the hands of the rulers. Yet when the end came, far from seeing that this was precisely what he had so constantly predicted, his disciples turned tail and fled back to Galilee in panic, without a seeming thought of waiting for the resurrection "after three days."

Had Jesus so believed and so spoken, it is incredible that his hearers could have been at one and the same time so cer-

[7] Luke 13:33.

[8] Mark 8:31–33; 9:30–32; 10:32–34; cf. Matt. 16:21–23; 17:22, 23; 20:17–19; Luke 9:22; 43b–45; 18:31–34.

[9] Mark 9:7; Matt. 17:5; Luke 9:35.

tain that as a prophet from God he was right, that all he said was God's own word, and yet so obtuse, so disbelieving, as to forsake him without awaiting the several-times-promised heavenly justification. And had Jesus himself so believed— whether due to assumed unique supernatural knowledge or as a part of what he believed God's message to him had entailed—there would seem little reason for the bleak moments of agony and uncertainty so poignantly revealed in the "great cry" on the cross, not to mention the dread night in Gethsemane's garden.

If, however, we are content to see Jesus convinced that he was the prophet of the new day—not, as his disciples subsequently came to believe, the instigator of it—many of these obscurities vanish. It is surely wise not to seek for a fictitious clarity at second or third remove. Whatever his precise motive, he turned toward Jerusalem—in Luke's unforgettable phrase, "he stedfastly set his face to go to Jerusalem" [10]—confident that God was directing his steps and consummating his purpose. While it was day, he must continue to work.

[10] Luke 9:51.

18

"O Jerusalem, Jerusalem, that killeth the prophets"

JESUS' ENTRY into Jerusalem sealed his doom. Rumors of the rabble-rousing, demon-possessed prophet with his message of the overthrow of law and order—exaggerated and garbled rumors and their credence by those in authority are no invention of the modern world—had preceded him. The audience in Jerusalem was vastly different from those made up largely of fishermen, artisans, and farmers in Galilee, and far less sympathetic. All the rumors they had heard must have seemed abundantly justified. Unless immediately checked, disaster was certain.

That the accounts we have of the "triumphal entry" or the "cleansing of the temple" are historical in the sense that either is a photograph of an actual event is unlikely. Jerusalem was a thoroughly policed city. In addition to the local police under the direction of the Sanhedrin—not to mention the very efficient temple police—the Roman governor, Pontius Pilate, was present with his troops, having come from his official residence in Cæsarea for the express purpose of seeing to it that the throngs in the city—for then as now, holy days were inevitably holidays—did not get out of bounds. There seems little reason to question that Jesus' arrival in Jerusalem was coincident—not improbably deliberately so—with the approaching Passover season.

That a demonstration such as is reported in ascending elaboration by all four evangelists,[1] with the prophet *riding into the city*, would have been tolerated is far from likely. In popular understanding, the fact that Jesus is reported to have ridden on an *ass* has been argued as a sign of humility: it was an *ass*, not a *war horse!* All this is most unjustified. The significant fact would be that he *rode* into the city, instead of dismounting and entering on foot. To ride in would be a claim to kingly power. That Rome would have tolerated it is utterly unlikely.

Nonetheless, although our stories clearly show the growth of tradition and are decked out now in appropriate biblical detail,[2] there may well be a solid kernel of fact, notably, the acclaim which the prophet received from pilgrims and city dwellers alike. That no Sadducees or Pharisees were to be seen in the noisy throng—at least as greeters!—would scarely need argument. The point is that the noisy and enthusiastic welcome extended to the prophet was his kiss of death, for it made evident, both to the native authorities in Jerusalem and to the Roman governor, the potential danger of a movement which might easily get out of hand.

The probability is that this menace seemed far greater to the Jewish authorities than to the Roman. As has already been remarked, during the early years of the Province of Judea there was actually far more authority in Jewish hands than in the preceding decades. Herod had been in name

---

[1] Mark 11:1–10; Matt. 21:1–9; Luke 19:28–38; John 12:12–19.
[2] The influence of Zech. 9:9 is unmistakable.

a Jewish king, though in the popular eye he was not only a paid tool of Rome but an Idumean in addition. It is very sure that during his long and able reign the local Sanhedrin had far less authority than it had enjoyed during the now almost fabled reign of Queen Salome (Alexander Jannæus' widow, Alexandra), who had astutely guarded herself from reaping the whirlwind her hated husband had sown. Nor during the short rule of Herod's son Archelaus had the native court enjoyed a free hand.

With the establishment of the new province at the time of Archelaus' deposition, matters changed. Rome remained supreme, but she acted through the local aristocracy. The Sanhedrin came to be the all-important source of both legislative and judicial action. But well did the leaders know that any indication of incompetence or lack of control which would endanger this small, but important, frontier province, would result in instant curbs. Thus the presence of a fanatic, whose one aim seemed to be to upset the *status quo* and who, worse yet, had already gained a large support from the lower classes, was not to be tolerated.

It is unlikely that the Pharisees, who constituted the religious leadership of the people, were as greatly concerned at this particular political or administrative menace as were the high priest and the Sanhedrin—in which latter body there is no real evidence that the Pharisees in those days were prominent. On the other hand, they were seemingly far from friendly or even indifferent. The contemptuous disregard of their all-important "tradition"—which naturally seemed a disregard for the scriptures themselves, for the tradition was but the explication of God's revelation in both Law and Prophets—was in their eyes little short of blasphemy. The very qualities which endeared Jesus to many of the common people, to whom the daily round was at best bare existence, with little of the privileges enjoyed by their betters, were but an additional offence in the eyes of those whose one concern was for what they fondly believed was true religion.

Jesus' easy pronouncements and judgments—to the prophet the natural and proper procedure of one whose lips God was moving—were to them the insolent and outrageous mouthings of an ignorant and untrained peasant, who not only was unforgivably destitute of the knowledge which God himself had enjoined upon all men as their chief duty, but who also blindly attacked them for doing what they knew was in strictest accord with God's clearly revealed will. His attraction to those who welcomed his words and shared his dreams, and which led the "common people to hear him gladly," but stamped him in the eyes of his opponents as a "friend of sinners"—birds of a feather flocking together. His disregard for such niceties as the twice-a-week fast—by no means universal in Judaism, even among the Pharisees themselves, but when contemptuously flouted, a lively source of indignation—and his careless hobnobbing at table with publicans and harlots gained for him the name, "a gluttonous man and a winebibber," [3] that is, he ate too heartily, drank too freely, and kept very disreputable company. In a word, when those responsible for the safety of the little state decided that this figure was a menace who must be speedily removed—"better one man perish than the nation" [4]—it could hardly be expected that he would find many vocal champions among the religiously and educationally elect.

One of the most persistent notes in the record of the final chapter in Jerusalem is that in which the temple is men-

[3] Matt. 11:19; Luke 7:34.　　　　[4] Cf. John 11:50; 18:14.

tioned. In the prelude to what is commonly styled "the little apocalypse," [5] and which in its present form cannot predate the dread year A.D. 70, which saw the destruction of the temple by the Roman general Titus, is the story that as Jesus left the temple he foretold its downfall, in answer to the word of one of his disciples, who was filled with awe at the huge stones with which it was built and which suggested its permanence: "Seest thou these great buildings? there shall not be left here one stone upon another, which shall not be thrown down." [6]

At the time of his arrest and inquisition false witnesses are represented as claiming that they had heard him say, "I will destroy this temple that is made with hands, and in three days I will build another made without hands." [7] As he hung on the cross, bystanders uttered the gibe: "Ha! thou that destroyest the temple, and buildest it in three days, save thyself, and come down from the cross." [8] In John, also, although at a place far earlier in the narrative, the same note is to be found: "Destroy this temple, and in three days I will raise it up." [9]

In addition, all four of the gospels have an account of Jesus overturning the tables of the money-changers and driving out the merchants and the animals they were offering for sale, with the indignant word: "Is it not written, My house shall be called a house of prayer for all the nations? but ye have made it a den of robbers." [10] Certainly as the

---

[5] As a consequence of the work of T. Colani and W. Weiffenbach the view has been widely accepted in critical circles that as the core of Mark 13 is to be seen an earlier Jewish or Jewish-Christian apocalypse. Opinions differ as to the precise nature and limits of this reworked earlier document, but most agree that verses 7–8, 14–20, and 24–27 are to be regarded an unretouched part of it.

[6] Mark 13:2; cf. Matt. 24:2 and Luke 21:6.

[7] Mark 14:58; cf. Matt. 26:61.

[8] Mark 15:29–30; cf. Matt. 27:39–40.   [9] John 2:19.

[10] Mark 11:17; Matt. 21:13; Luke 19:46; cf. John 2:16.

account stands in Mark it was this act which crystalized the leaders' wrath and led to his speedy arrest and death.

Despite the patent difficulties in all this material as we have it, and the presence of details easier to be explained as coming from a much later date—the persistent joining of the time element, "after three days," to the prediction; the amazing escape of Jesus, unmolested by the temple police, after an act so easily construed as one of wanton violence in a sacred shrine—it is impossible to escape the conclusion that prominent among the words actually spoken by Jesus while in Jerusalem were passionate denunciations of what the temple had become and a prediction of its speedy downfall.

As to whether the "cleansing of the temple" was an actual act by Jesus or an enacted parable, in which, in the course of the years, another "And he said" came to be turned by easy metamorphosis into an "And he did," is not easy to decide at our remove, and competent scholars have differed widely.

The obvious difficulty lies in the amazing restraint of the temple police in permitting such an act. However a later age may view it, in the view of the authorities it would have been nothing short of sacrilege, and sacrilege was an offense by no means lightly condoned. The Roman governor would almost certainly have been quick to act in such a case, if appealed to by the authorities, for Rome was adamant in her unwillingness to allow matters religious to become matters political.

On the other hand, there is another aspect to the affair which may well be pondered: the nature of the traffic in the temple court with which Jesus is represented as interfering so forthrightly. There can be but little question but what the traffic was in connection with sacrifices and offerings. Sacrificial victims must be ceremonially proper—that is, free from defects or blemishes. Offerings of money must be in the sacred currency no longer easily available in trade. To meet these needs both acceptable animals and currency were available for convenient purchase. Naturally, it was far more convenient, especially for pilgrims from a distance, to purchase a victim on the spot. And there was always the possibility that an animal brought by the worshiper himself might be technically disqualified. All of this traffic was under the control of the priests, and the profits were very considerable. It is not surprising that to many pilgrims these services (for which, of course, a charge was made) were annoying and easily construed as evidences of graft, especially when private animals were disqualified simply because of trivial and, in the eyes of the owners, quite imaginary defects.

Accordingly, the act of Jesus, as recounted in the familiar story, might well be vociferously applauded by many a pilgrim as the God-inspired correction of an obvious abuse. Thus the menace to the authorities, and their dilemma. Whatever they did would be wrong. If unpunished, the act could spell the end of a very lucrative source of income. If Jesus, on the other hand, were to be arrested by the temple police, it might well lead to an instant riot on the part of the crowds who would seek to defend their martyred champion. A riot would be disastrous. Pilate with his guard was hard by the temple in the tower of Antonia, prepared for precisely such an emergency. Roman intervention would be fatal. Not only might it lead to drastic curtailment of local control, which in Roman eyes would now be judged ineffective; it would inevitably lead to profanation of the courts of the temple by the despised foreigners, who might very well

be less than scrupulous, once there on official business, in
observing the proprieties and honoring the boundaries beyond which no gentile might go.

In consequence, the story which, when first read, seems
so unlikely, can conceivably have more than a kernel of fact
behind it. On the other hand, it is perhaps more likely as an
"enacted parable," reflecting Jesus' manifest and outspoken
hostility to all that the temple had come to represent. Surely
the sweating hosts of pilgrims surging through its courts,
the lowing and bellowing of terrified cattle in the pens and
on the slabs for slaughter; the billowing clouds of smoke
and the nauseous stench from burning fat and meat; the cries
of hawkers and money-changers—all this might have seemed
to an even less sensitive observer than the prophet from
Nazareth, little accustomed to such tumult and superficial
piety, a strange answer to the age-old query of a Micah:

> Wherewith shall I come before Yahweh, and bow myself be-
> fore the high God? shall I come before him with burnt-offerings,
> with calves a year old? will Yahweh be pleased with thousands
> of rams, or with ten thousands of rivers of oil? shall I give my
> first-born for my transgression, the fruit of my body for the sin
> of my soul? He hath showed thee, O man, what is good; and what
> doth Yahweh require of thee, but to do justly, and to love kind-
> ness, and to walk humbly with thy God? [11]

To the outraged eyes of the prophet from Nazareth he
was but once more joining the ranks of the host of earlier
prophets whom God had raised up, as he uttered his blasts
against this sorry perversion of Israel's greatest obligation
and privilege. With his overpowering confidence that the
new age was speedily to dawn, and that its dawn would
bring the blotting out of all that made the present age one
of evil, it would not be surprising that the temple—strange

[11] Micah 6:6–8.

anachronism of the past—should seem, just because of its arrogant aspect of permanence, the symbol of what was doomed to pass. In the new age there might well be a temple where God would dwell among his people; but it would be a temple vastly different from this one with its greedy priests and stinking smells.

Such an attack, though unaccompanied by the incidental gesture of overturning tables, was unforgivable. It at once clarifies the whole story. Of course his doom was sealed, and the justification of his removal rendered easy. The charge of blasphemy, which the high priest is reported by Mark to have brought against him,[12] has seemed to many readers surprising, for it is made to follow Jesus' affirmation to the query: "Art thou the Christ, the Son of the Blessed?" Such a claim might seem to his enemies insolent. It surely was not blasphemy. Blasphemy was "cursing God by the name of God." [13]

But with the removal of this claim—at least in the sense that "anointed" subsequently acquired—the difficulty vanishes. If, as these constant references to the temple and its speedy destruction suggest, Jesus had inveighed against the temple and its deeply entrenched coterie of wealthy priests and supporters, the charge of blasphemy was less unnatural. In the eyes of the priests and their retainers attacks upon the temple were an attack upon God. It was his residence, the embodiment of his presence. Jeremiah might have told a vivid story of what had resulted when he, six centuries before had cried out in the name of the Lord: "Therefore will I do unto the house which is called by my name, wherein ye trust, and unto the place which I gave to you and to your fathers, as I did to Shiloh." [14] As a consequence, the verdict in the

---

[12] Mark 14:64; cf. Matt. 26:65.   [13] Mishnah Sanhedrin 7, 5.
[14] Jer. 7:14; cf. 26:6.

case of Jeremiah, precisely as it is reported of Jesus, was: "This man is worthy of death; for he hath prophesied against this city, as ye have heard with your ears." [15]

Thus it appears to me very probable that the prompt action of the Jewish authorities—the speedy arrest of Jesus and his immediate condemnation; the report to the Roman governor, charging the prisoner with "sedition" and incitement of the mob, both of which were punishable under Roman law by crucifixion—was occasioned by Jesus' passionate avowal that the axe was already laid at the root of the tree and that the end of the present order was at hand, for this in the eyes of the authorities was a direct attack upon both state and temple. And the fact that he was no remote or solitary figure—no voice of one crying in the wilderness—but had come, as they were convinced, with a throng of followers to Jerusalem for the express purpose of inciting the mob of pilgrims to violence, only added to their fears and fury.

This provided an easy out for the Jewish authorities. Regardless of the endlessly debated and still uncertain question of whether the Sanhedrin did or did not have the right of inflicting capital punishment during the decade of Pilate's governorship, here was an offense which either was, or could easily be represented to be, manifestly in the field of Rome's immediate concern. The Roman law was clear: "Persons who cause sedition or upheaval or who incite the mobs are, depending upon their civic status, liable to crucifixion, or to be thrown to the wild beasts, or to be banished to an island." [16]

[15] Jer. 26:11.

[16] *Actores [auctores, P] seditionis et tumultus populo concitato [vel concitatores populi, P] pro qualitate dignitatis aut in furcam [crucem, P] tolluntur aut bestiis obiciuntur aut in insulam deportantur—Digesta* xxxxviii, 19, 38, 2. This section of the Justinian Pandects is quoted (with slight alterations) from the third-century jurist, Julius Paulus (v, 22, 1). That the threefold distinction of penalties was in effect at the time of the execution of Jesus is improbable, and the types of penalties seem clearly to be of

One of the most conspicuous elements in the book of Acts is the apologetic emphasis. This is readily understandable. As the movement, which eventually came to be and to be known as Christianity, spread out into the Roman world, among the greatest obstacles which it faced was the suspicion of being a subversive, anti-Roman movement. This became even more acute as the new movement came to be regarded as distinct from Judaism and thus deprived of the latter's privilege as a recognized and tolerated religion (*religio licita*).

There were many things which made it suspect. The fact that its central message was the dawn of the new "kingdom," for a kingdom not unnaturally suggested a king. Another danger signal was the fact that its leader had been crucified at the order of the Roman governor. That could not be denied; it must be explained away. Thus the emphasis grew that it was utterly against the desire of Pilate that the terrible deed was done. Repeatedly he had stated his opinion that Jesus was innocent. Mark's perplexed question, "Why, what evil hath he done?" and the manifest hope that he might release Jesus and execute Barabbas,[17] become progressively heightened. In Matthew[18] it has reached a climax. Pilate knows that Jesus is innocent, and washes his hands in dramatic fashion: "I am innocent of the blood of this righteous man; see ye to it." His wife had had a dream—a heavenly apparition—the night before, which she hastily reported to

---

the later age. However, it is highly probable that crucifixion was, then as later, the normal penalty for non-Roman citizens guilty of the offense. Under the influence of Christianity, which had taken the cross as its proud symbol, crucifixion was abolished in the later years of Constantine, but not for humane reasons. This accounts for the alteration of Paulus' *crucem* (cross) to *furcam* (fork). For a discussion of crucifixion and of sedition, see T. Mommsen, *Römisches Strafrecht*, pp. 918–921 and 562–565.

[17] Mark 15:6–15.   [18] Matt. 27:15–26.

her husband in the attempt to prevent his folly. In the Apocryphal Gospel of Peter, Pilate is completely exonerated: it was the Jews and the Jews alone who were guilty.[19] Further consideration of this aspect may be for the moment deferred. The significant element is the manifest attempt to allay Roman suspicion in the larger Roman world into which the movement was spreading.

So in the other accounts in Acts. Again and again the leaders had been arrested. It was always, however, unwarranted and due to Jewish malice. Heavenly release, as in the repeated experiences of Peter and John,[20] and of Paul at Philippi; [21] Roman officials recognizing the innocence of the arrested man and apologizing for their unwarranted action; the Roman governor in Corinth, Gallio, refusing to aid the Jews in their plot against a man innocent of any offence recognized by Rome [22]—this note is too persistent to be accidental.

Against this background—and I have listed but a few of the many bits of evidence—the accounts in the gospels linking Jesus with the temple may with profit be re-examined. The mention of the rebuilding within or after three days, already noted, arouses the suspicion that here is a palpable reflection of the resurrection confidence and that we thus have essentially a pun: the temple has now become the temple which was his body. Actually in John this is directly affirmed: "But he spake of the temple of his body." [23] So common did this figure of speech become that in the Markan

---

[19] The fragment begins: "... but of the Jews none washed his hands, neither Herod nor any of his judges. And when they wished to wash them, Pilate rose up. And then Herod the king [sic] commanded that the Lord be taken, saying to them: What things soever I commanded you to do unto him, do" (Gospel of Peter 1).

[20] Acts 5:17–32; 12:1–19.   [21] Acts 16:19–40.
[22] Acts 18:12–17.   [23] John 2:21.

passage where Jesus prophesies the destruction of the temple, in answer to the comment of the awed disciple, two manuscripts (D and W) actually add "and after three days another shall arise without hands." [24]

It is well worth considering whether this identification of "temple" as "temple of his body" was not a deliberate attempt to remove from his words an emphasis which could easily be construed as sanctioning, if not inciting, violence, even rebellion. Furthermore, it can hardly be due to accident that in Luke's parallels to Mark 14:58 and 15:29—the report of the false witnesses concerning Jesus' threat and the gibe of the bystanders at the cross—all mention of the word against the temple is absent. Again, in Luke's very brief mention of the cleansing of the temple,[25] Mark's vivid story of the overturned tables and benches and the refusal to allow any man to carry a vessel through the temple is drastically shortened and presented without trace of violence. Certainly the apologetic note so manifest in Acts is also present in that same author's "first volume," our Gospel of Luke. The author is very careful to omit any touch which might warrant the view that Jesus died as a malefactor. Instead he died as the Messiah.

That a similar concern led the author of the Fourth Gospel to place the cleansing of the temple early in his narrative [26] and to substitute for it the raising of Lazarus from the dead as the real cause of Jesus' arrest, would seem to me far from unlikely.

In this connection a final word may be added. It would

[24] Mark 13:2.   [25] Luke 19:45–48.

[26] The popular impression that the two incidents are distinct and that John's is an earlier ("first") cleansing is, of course, quite in error and a residuum of the view that the Fourth Gospel, like the Synoptists, is a proper source for historical reconstruction and can be braided in with them to give a composite picture.

appear to me possible, even probable, that our stories of the
cleansing of the temple are themselves a deliberate revision
and toning down of an earlier tradition in which Jesus'
strictures on the temple and all for which it stood were far
more direct and unqualified than in these stories in which his
animus is limited to one abuse under which the temple was
suffering. If this possibility be considered seriously, the form
of the story which has replaced the repeated sweeping denunciations may well have been suggested by the word of
Jeremiah: "Is this house, which is called by my name, become a den of robbers in your eyes?" [27]

[27] Jer. 7:11.

19

"And delivered him up to Pilate"

T̲H̲E̲ D̲E̲T̲A̲I̲L̲S̲ of the arrest, trial, and conviction of Jesus, despite vivid and at times seeming first-hand reports, are at best uncertain. Some matters would seem sure. The official condemnation to death and the resulting execution by crucifixion were at the hands of Rome, through her local governor, Pontius Pilate. On the other hand, it appears equally certain that Pilate's action was not due to his own initiative, but was the result of the pressure upon him by the Jewish authorities, who not unnaturally had speedily apprehended Jesus and lost little time in effecting the desired sentence of death.

When one seeks to fill in the details and reconstruct the series of successive scenes, he finds himself faced with obscurities and uncertainties which cannot be resolved. In the first place, what reliable sources do we have? In the several gospel accounts—actually we have two: the one in Mark, somewhat altered and recast by Matthew and Luke; the other in John, which is basically so different that it seems impossible to see it as simply derived from the other—are many touches, which when superficially read, seem as if taken down by a reporter with notebook and pencil. We read the precise words of the principals in, so to speak, direct quotes.

What is the source of this information? Surely none of the followers of Jesus was present. It is scarcely likely that those in authority made such reports subsequently available. We easily overlook the manifold difficulties here, as well as in Gethsemane's garden, where a verbatim account of the words of Jesus' prayers is given, although all who could report them were seemingly themselves asleep.

It was precisely because there were no official reports available—either Jewish or Roman—that Christians attempted to fill in these gaps, to them so obvious and intolerable. The result was the production of purely imaginative "official reports." Justin Martyr, writing in the second century, can casually refer his readers to the official Acts reporting the trial of Jesus in the Roman archives. It is not that Justin had seen them. Rather, it is to him incomprehensible that so world-shaking an event should not have received full and detailed official treatment. This feeling of Justin's was shared by many other Christians as the years went by, and pious, if clumsy, attempts were made to fill in—or "make available"—the to them certain details. Another reason which may well have led to the composition by Christians of such documents as the *Acts of Pilate* [1] was the desire to counteract and nullify false "Acts," which hostile pagans were producing and seeking to introduce into the schools in the early fourth century.

The question of the availability to Christians of reliable sources of information about the trial of Jesus cannot be brushed aside. To be sure, the accounts in the gospels are

[1] A translation of the fourth-century apocryphon is conveniently available in M. R. James, *The Apocryphal New Testament*, pp. 94–165.

vivid, but upon what are they based? Is it upon a factual
report of what actually transpired, for the most part behind
closed doors, and provided by those who were present, or
upon a rapidly growing popular tradition which sought to
fill in the colorful details which simply were not available?
It is at this point that the historian's reticence and caution
are particularly unwelcome to many readers, to whom they
seem unwarranted, if not actually supercilious: "The Bible
is different from all other books and is itself its own guarantee."

Together with this difficulty is another, itself so surcharged
with emotion that a dispassionate survey of the confused
evidence and a readiness to accept what would seem to be
fact regardless of its nature is for many impossible. For Jews
the matter is no mere academic or literary problem. Due to
what may soberly be called an historical accident—although
to many Christians that term will seem far from adequate—
the death of Jesus has come to assume a magnitude of significance without parallel in human history. Many other men
—noble men—have died, and at the hands of their fellow
countrymen; some have been remembered and honored,
notably Socrates, but without the emotional overtones consequent upon Calvary. Socrates did not speedily come to be
regarded as the divine founder of the one true religion; nor
were his fellow Greeks who put him away regarded as responsible leaders of another religion which too continued as
a world-wide cult.

That makes all the difference in the world. There are some
—in terms of statistics unfortunately very few—to whom
Socrates is more than a name, and who cannot read the accounts of his death with dry eyes. But Socrates, however
much they revere him, is not regarded, even by them, as the
founder of their religion, and they are not confronted by a

host in another world religion—with whom they daily rub elbows—who pride themselves on being heirs of those whose leaders forced upon Socrates the deadly hemlock. Thus we can honor Socrates with no rankling question, "Who put him to death?" and with no hostility at all for the archons of Athens or even the reluctant jailer.

In the case of Jesus of Nazareth and his Jewish foes the matter is utterly different. For nineteen centuries the epithet "Christ killer" has been applied without discrimination to members of the other religion, solely because they were Jews. It is beyond the scope of the present volume to attempt to review that story or even to list many other factors which are of importance and too often overlooked. It must, however, be insisted that the manifest, if understandable, attempt which had arisen well before the end of the first century to ascribe to the Jews a prime responsibility for the death of Jesus, an attempt which is so clear in the added Matthæan details of the trial, climaxed by the awful shout, "His blood be upon us, and on our children" [2]—which dreadful word is not ascribed to the high priest and his coterie but to "all the people"!—has borne a bitter fruit. Begging for the moment our main question, it should be said that this ascription to "all the people" is scarcely factual.

The aim attributed by Mark to the "chief priests and scribes" to "take him with subtlety, and kill him: for they said, Not during the feast, lest haply there shall be a tumult of the people," [3] would seem historically probable, even though events proved such that the act was actually consummated during the feast. This latter fact apparently led Luke to revise Mark at this point and to reserve the unfulfilled "not during the feast" for his story of the subsequent

[2] Matt. 27:25.   [3] Mark 14:1, 2.

arrest of Peter.[4] Furthermore, the impression in the stories of hasty proceedings, in part to anticipate the time of necessary inaction when once the feast had begun, suggests the not unwarranted fear that any delay might well lead to dreaded riots and even an attempted jail delivery, which would have resulted in precisely what the authorities feared most—prompt intervention by Pilate.

One final word is long overdue: Without regard to the number of Jews who may have approved that drastic act in the long distant month of Nisan, it is without rational warrant—not to say Christian decency—to continue to visit upon the heads of remote descendants responsibility for an act which, while unwise and uncalled for, *as later events have seemed to prove it to be,* may well have seemed to those who so acted highly proper and necessary, both for the cause of Israel and of God. The popular picture of both the Jewish leaders and Pilate deliberately doing what they knew was wicked is stupidly perverse. Those today who have a hatred of revolutionary violence and a feeling of responsibility for keeping intact the "American way of life," may well thank God that it was not their fate to have lived in Jerusalem in A.D. 29. Without the vista of the past nineteen hundred years, it could well have been that some of the most orthodox today, had they been there then, would have approved the sorry verdict.

That Jesus was arrested by a posse sent by what can be loosely styled the "Jewish government" would seem probable. Some of the other details in the story may well appear far less certain. That he was arrested as an insurrectionist is certainly implied by the term translated "robber" (λῃστής).

[4] Luke 22:1-2; Acts 12:1-19, (cf. especially v.4).

This is the word in Jesus' indignant protest: "Are ye come out, as against a *robber*, with swords and staves to seize me?"[5] It is the term used not only of the two others crucified with Jesus[6] but also by John in description of Barabbas,[7] whom Luke characterizes as "one who for a certain insurrection made in the city, and for murder, was cast into prison."[8] The word would appear the common term used by their opponents for those accused of revolutionary violence. There may well have been many, like Josephus, who so viewed and styled those men who, in their own thinking, were one hundred percent patriots. That Jesus shared the views of the "fourth philosophy," is, as has been already remarked, most improbable. Nonetheless, his denunciation of the temple and his confidence that it, along with all other abuses, was speedily to fall, may well have led to an inexact and quite unwarranted view of him, and an easy identification of him as a "red." Today many holding the most diverse views, political and religious, are lumped together by their several opponents as "reds." There seems little reason for assuming that this is a new or novel procedure.

The part played by Judas Iscariot in the betrayal and arrest is far from certain. The common explanation has been that he acted as guide to the secluded garden. Occasionally, some, notably Schweitzer, have seen in Judas' word to the authorities the disclosure, not of Jesus' whereabouts, but of Jesus' claims for himself, which he had permitted only his immediate inner circle of followers—Peter, James, and John —to learn, and which Peter had rashly blurted out in the presence of the rest, of whom Judas was one.[9] But at best

[5] Mark 14:48.   [6] Mark 15:27; Matt. 27:38.   [7] John 18:40.
[8] Luke 23:19; cf. 23:25.
[9] Schweitzer (*The Quest of the Historical Jesus,* pp. 380–384; 394 f.) thus reverses the Markan order of Peter's confession and the Transfiguration. Rather, it was on the mountainside that "in a state of rapture common

all this is the sheerest speculation, as is the theory that Judas had acted in the best of faith, to force Jesus to make public a claim, certain that it would win immediate support and assure complete God-given triumph to Jesus himself. In later thinking the question of why a traitor should have been selected by Jesus in the first place became troublesome. Since Jesus had supernatural knowledge, he was, of course, not only aware that Judas would so act,[10] but, for reasons best known to himself and God, had elected Judas with foreknowledge and deliberation.

The site of the arrest, in Gethsemane on the side of the Mount of Olives, raises even more serious queries. The impression from Mark, followed by Matthew, is that this was the first time Jesus had gone to this spot. He knew that the end was at hand, and had sought out the secluded place with quiet deliberation. Superficially, this might seem to make Judas' rôle as a guide the more probable. But questions at once arise. How did Judas know, several days in advance, that at the chosen hour Jesus would be precisely here? And why the need of identifying Jesus among his few companions by the kiss? There would seem little reason to suppose that Jesus, even after but a short stop in the city, would be unknown by face to the authorities.[11]

Luke has slightly altered the situation. Regularly Jesus had spent the night on the Mount of Olives—"And every day he was teaching in the temple; *and every night* he went out, and lodged in the mount that is called Olivet." [12] So

---

to them all" Peter had learned the secret, and subsequently had divulged it to the rest of the Twelve.

[10] John 6:64 and 71; 13:11.

[11] At any rate, the overtheatric gesture of the kiss by Judas would appear to evidence one bit more of the growing tradition about the traitor rather than to be an unretouched detail of the actual event.

[12] Luke 21:37.

when he left the upper room on the fatal evening for Olivet it was "as his custom was." [13] This might explain how Judas knew the likely spot; it also raises the question as to why a guide for the police should be necessary.

A more serious problem for the historian is raised by the story of a similar experience of David.[14] In David's flight from Absalom he had left Jerusalem to escape the conspiracy against his life, crossed the brook Kidron and ascended the Mount of Olives, and "he wept as he went up." Among his company was a traitor, Ahithophel; on the way David was stoned and cursed by Shimei, the son of Gera. It is hard to avoid the feeling that early Christians, who knew this story, saw in it a parallel to an incident in the life of "Great David's greater son." To what extent our gospel stories of this incident are based on eyewitness tradition, to what extent they are colored by, if not directly dependent upon, the earlier incident, cannot be determined with precision. The feeling persists that there is a very definite literary connection and that without the earlier biblical story of David's flight the form of the gospel story might well have been different.

According to the account in Mark, which appears to be the sole literary source for Matthew's and Luke's versions, Jesus was conducted at once to the high priest. It was, according to the account, a far from private session, for the high priest had assembled "all the chief priests and the elders and the scribes." [15] It was at this session that the "chief priests and the whole council" [16] made use of the false witnesses and eventually reached the conclusion: "worthy of death for blasphemy." Early the next morning "the chief priests with the elders and scribes, and the whole council, held a consultation, and bound Jesus, and carried him away,

---

[13] Luke 22:39.   [14] II Sam. 15–16.   [15] Mark 14:53.
[16] οἱ δὲ ἀρχιερεῖς καὶ ὅλον τὸ συνέδριον—Mark 14:55.

and delivered him up to Pilate."[17] In this laconic account it is impossible to be sure of details. Were there two sessions of the same group? Were either or both sessions of the "Sanhedrin," or is the Greek word συνέδριον used in the less technical sense of a different (less formal) "council"? Was the second meeting to confirm the earlier decision or was it for the purpose of accomplishing the demanded death, by referring the matter to the Roman governor? Did they decide on the accusation of Jesus: he has claimed to be the king; or was this Pilate's own conclusion about the "robber" brought before him for his decision?

Luke has varied the Markan account in a conspicuous detail. He has but one meeting of the council—"And as soon as it was day, the assembly of the elders of the people was gathered together, both chief priests and scribes; and they led him away into their council (*synedrion*). . . ."[18] Luke seems to feel that during the preceding night Jesus was held by the posse which had arrested him. It was *they,* not the "council" as Mark had implied, that subjected him to the brutal horseplay. Instead of a second meeting of the Jewish "council" Luke tells of a session before Herod Antipas, who chanced to be in Jerusalem, and to whom Pilate sent Jesus after learning that he was a Galilean.[19]

That any of these Lucan modifications indicate another and non-Markan source, upon which Luke is drawing, would seem unlikely, although frequently postulated. The vulgar brutality which Jesus suffered may well have seemed to Luke, as it has to many a subsequent reader, incredible at the hands of the "council." Instead he transfers it to the guards. It was this session before Herod Antipas, quite unnoticed by Mark, which was the occasion for the dressing of Jesus in mock royal robes and for the insults, which Mark

[17] Mark 15:1.   [18] Luke 22:66.   [19] Luke 23:6–16.

had listed as done by the Romans after Pilate's sentence.[20] The source of this trial before Herod would seem an early Christian (Lucan?) inference. Did not Psalm 2 refer to "the *kings* of the earth *and the rulers* in array against the Lord and against his Anointed"? That Luke regarded this as apt in connection with Jesus' death is made certain by his quotation and interpretation of it in a speech by Peter and John in Acts.[21]

In this fog of uncertainty as to precise details of the measures against Jesus which resulted in his remand to Pilate are several other matters which remain most obscure. All of them are closely twined together and have to do with the "council." The first of these is: Did the Sanhedrin have the power to pass and carry into execution the death sentence for any offense? Here scholarly opinion is far from unanimous. The Gospel of John flatly denies the authority: "The Jews said unto him [*sc.* Pilate], 'It is not lawful for us to put any man to death.'"[22] The laconic statement of Josephus, often cited in this connection, is far from clear: "And now Archelaus' part of Judea was reduced into a province, and Coponius, one of the equestrian order among the Romans, was sent as a procurator, *having the power of life and death put into his hands by Cæsar.*"[23] Some interpret this word as meaning that authority to pronounce and execute a death sentence was limited to the procurator, and that, by implication, the Sanhedrin's authority was thus restricted. Other scholars, convinced on other grounds that the Sanhedrin did possess the authority to pass a death sentence, would understand Josephus to mean that the Roman governor's authority included this power too, but without excluding the right of the Sanhedrin to handle (at least some) capital cases.

[20] Mark 15:16–20; so Matt. 27:27–31.
[21] Acts 4:25 ff.; cf. also Matt. 10:18.　　　　[22] John 18:31.
[23] Josephus, *Wars* 2, 8, 1.

To me the evidence is far from conclusive. The case of Stephen's death,[24] often cited, is at best uncertain. Was this a formal execution? Was it a lynching? From the account in Acts we simply do not know. And the same can be said for certain other often-cited cases: the burning of the high priest's daughter who was convicted of adultery,[25] and the stoning of James.[26] The signs in the temple courtyard warning foreigners of the death penalty which would be their certain fate should they pass beyond the prescribed limits are of little help here.[27] That the penalty would be automatic is probable, but at whose hands is not indicated. When Roman procurators succeeded the house of Herod, did they become the agents for the execution? We simply do not know.

To be sure, this, like many other details, would seem to be far less perplexing in the light of the full and detailed accounts of the procedures of the Sanhedrin in the Mishnah tract by the same name. Here we have detailed rules for judicial action: the methods of conducting trials, the restrictions upon witnesses, the lapse of time before pronouncing sentence, the several forms of execution which could be inflicted (burning, stoning, strangling, beheading), and many other related matters. It is in the light of this compendium of practices that studies of the trial of Jesus have often been attempted, especially by lawyers, with particular attention to the query: was the trial of Jesus, by contemporary Jewish practice, legal?

This raises the second of the intertwined problems: Do the tract Sanhedrin in the Mishnah and the related sources pro-

---

[24] Acts 7:54–8:1.   [25] Mishnah Sanhedrin 7, 2.
[26] Josephus, *Antt.* 20, 9, 1; Eusebius, *Hist. Eccl.* ii, 23, 1–18.
[27] These signs are mentioned by Josephus (*Antt.* 5, 5, 2) as being prominently displayed in Greek and Latin. A pillar carrying the following (Greek) inscription was unearthed in 1871: "No foreigner is to enter within the balustrade and embankment around the sacred place; whoever is caught will be responsible for his death which will follow."

vide us with information as to the make-up and procedure of
the Sanhedrin in the days when it did have definite authority
and power? One of the consequences of the Jewish war
against Rome (A.D. 66–73) was the end of the Sanhedrin as
an authoritative organ of government. Somewhat after the
debacle the doctors of the law established at near-by Jamnia
a so-called Court of Justice, styled in Jewish practice *Bet
Din*, which they believed to be a continuation of the Sanhedrin, and which was accordingly read back to the days of
Moses, in accord with the principle so central to Jewish
confidence. This new *Bet Din*, quite regardless of its own
theories about its unaltered continuity from the remote past,
was simply a rabbinical assembly, with no legal authority
to carry out its decisions. It was a body of scribes, headed by
the chief teachers of Israel. Since it had no authority, save
that of influence, its practices and procedures could and did
become purely academic.

The detailed and romantic picture in the Mishnah tract
of this leisurely group of pundits debating such scarcely
contemporary problems as the rights and limitations of the
king, has been uncritically accepted by occasional lawyers,
who thus believed they had found proof positive of the
illegal procedure taken against Jesus. Did not the Mishnah
insist that there be a lapse of thirty days before pronouncement of the death sentence? Was it not illegal in a capital
case to find a prisoner guilty if the adverse vote had been
unanimous? Both of these details were shockingly invalidated
in the case of Jesus. Therefore the trial of Jesus was illegal
even by Jewish standards.

But this picture of the *Bet Din* throws little or no light
on the practices and procedures of the earlier body which
had been geared for action and invested with a direct authority for the conduct of the life of the province. Unlike the

later "law school," whose members sat in a semicircle "like the half of a round threshing floor so that all might see one another," with three rows of students on the front benches for instruction, and with the high priest far from being its presiding officer but rather subject to all its regulations, the "earlier" Sanhedrin had had a membership in which the priestly group with Sadducean sympathies had constituted a majority, although seemingly some from the ranks of the Pharisees were also to be found, and with the high priest its presiding officer.

Attempts have been made, notably by Adolf Büchler [28] and Solomon Zeitlin,[29] to justify the Bet Din's fond belief that as it was, so the Sanhedrin had always been, by assuming two bodies: the *religious* Sanhedrin, essentially as pictured in the later rabbinical sources, which was concerned solely with jurisdiction over religious matters, independent of the civil power, with authority to carry out its carefully safeguarded verdicts of death; and the *political* Sanhedrin, under the headship of the high priest, who could convene his carefully hand-picked cohort of supporters whenever a man was accused of committing a crime against the state or of a nature to offend the ruler.

Thus in the eyes of Zeitlin it was the latter group—essentially a group of Quislings—who were responsible for the arrest, mock trial, and railroading of Jesus. The Jewish people, who in Zeitlin's eyes are seen not unnaturally as essentially Pharisees, were in no sense responsible for the arrest and death of Jesus. It was the Roman, not the Jew, who was responsible, for the high priest and his supporters were simply Roman yes men.

[28] A. Büchler, *Das Synedrion in Jerusalem und das grosse Bet-Din in der Quaderkammer des jerusalemischen Tempels.*
[29] S. Zeitlin, *Who Crucified Jesus?* pp. 68–83.

The difficulty with this view, as I see it, is twofold: the lack of real evidence for these two distinct bodies, and the constant reference to "chief priests, elders, and scribes" in the body, whatever its actual nature, which was responsible for the verdict and subsequent arraignment before Pilate. Therefore, to me, attempts to analyze the gospel stories of the trial and to discuss them in terms of what is fondly called "the legal proceedings of the Sanhedrin" are for the most part worthless.[30] That Jesus was arrested and speedily remanded to the Roman governor for condemnation and execution as a man whose words and actions were dangerous to the state would seem as certain as the elaborating details are obscure.

[30] On the contrary, the volume, *Who Crucified Jesus?* by Solomon Zeitlin, may be studied with great profit, even if one finds Zeitlin's contention of the "*religious* Sanhedrin" a reading back and reflection of the Bet Din. For students anxious to sound these rock-filled waters, the article, "Marginal Notes on the Trial of Jesus," by Paul Winter, in *Zeitschrift für die neutestamentliche Wissenschaft*, Vol. 50, parts 1–2 and 3–4 (1959), is to be commended as sane and rewarding.

20

"And Pilate answered"

Estimates of Pontius Pilate are by no means easy. That his was the voice which sent Jesus to the cross would seem a plain fact. "Suffered under Pontius Pilate, was crucified, dead, and buried" is one item in an ancient creed which no historian will likely question. And for many who repeat this statement it is quite sufficient to warrant the common verdict of Pilate's unqualified guilt. The fact that in the several gospels he is represented as the unwilling tool of those who had remanded their prisoner to him but heightens his guilt. He knew that the prisoner was innocent and sought in vain to free himself from the responsibility of executing an innocent man. His cowardly fear of personal reprisals, should he not yield, forced him, wide-eyed, to act as he did.

That this conventional drawing is in no sense an untouched photograph, or even a true portrait, but rather a gross caricature of the luckless procurator of Judea, it would seem impossible to deny. It is not difficult to discern the reasons which led the early artists to depict him as they did. That the results were *natural* is far from saying that they were *true.* Rather, they were the inevitable result of a twofold desire: on the one hand, to prove the political innocence of the Christian movement in the eyes of Rome by the very effective claim, "Your own governor who condemned him knew that he was innocent"; on the other, hostility to the Jews, whom Christians were finding, now that the ways between Synagogue and Church had so definitely parted, among their bitterest enemies.[1]

Actually we know very little about Pilate save that he was kept in office by Tiberius for ten years (A.D. 26–36). That in itself is no mean recommendation, for Tiberius kept a very close watch upon his border provinces and accepted no excuses from governors unfortunate enough to incur his suspicion of mismanagement. Our information as to details of those ten years is small, and is provided by two writers, Josephus and Philo, both of whom reported the particular incidents for very different purposes. Josephus is eager to illustrate his thesis that the real reason the naturally tractable and friendly Jews had rebelled against Rome, was the fact that the governors whom Rome had sent were far from representative, but had been a group of increasingly cruel and rapacious scoundrels, who had needlessly exasperated the nation and had made it increasingly easy for irresponsible troublemakers to arouse their more sober countrymen. Philo mentions Pilate solely to add an additional support to his thesis that the Jews are the most loyal subjects in the empire and that governors who injure them do so at their peril. Pilate, like others in Alexandria, had sought to act in

---

[1] At the time our gospels—especially the three later ones—were produced, Sadducees and chief priests had for the most part dropped out of sight. When their temple fell in A.D. 70, they fell with it. It is surely not surprising that in the gospels we find the "scribes and Pharisees"—who had continued, as the others had not—the chief recipients of attacks and woes. These were the Jews with whom the churches were in contact and whom they were finding their foe.

a manner which was suicidal. The emperor, having been informed of his governor's reckless act, had at once peremptorily rebuked him and had righted the wrong. Thus in both cases the stories are very definitely slanted.

A sober reading of the three incidents which these protagonists were able to dredge up seem to indicate that, as might well have been expected, Pilate had found himself at a constant loss to understand the people he was expected to govern. It was for precisely this reason, it may be interjected, that Augustus had earlier preferred, whenever possible, native governors who knew the local situation as no foreigner could and who would then be able to prevent zeal for local folkways taking on a dangerous political aspect if unwisely or unnecessarily checked.

Early in his term of office Pilate had sent troops to Jerusalem. Naturally they had carried with them, as Roman troops normally would, standards bearing Tiberius' image. There had been no problem over this in Cæsarea, but in near-by Jerusalem they produced such a furore that a delegation from that city had come to the governor in Cæsarea, to demand the removal of the offensive flags. For five days the Jerusalemites had refused to yield although immediate execution had been threatened.[2]

At another time Pilate had started to construct an aqueduct to give Jerusalem a decent water supply. A howling mob was the result of what must have seemed to the Roman a most natural and beneficial undertaking. The fact that to aid in financing the necessarily costly construction he had used some of the money stored in the temple, instead of attempting to levy a more direct tax, may well have seemed to the governor a most normal procedure. In many provinces it would probably have been accepted without especial com-

[2] Josephus, *Wars* 2, 9, 2–3; *Antt.* 18, 3, 1.

ment. In Jerusalem it was very different, and it required soldiers to dispel the wrathful crowds.[3]

The one incident reported by Philo is so similar to that of the standards that it may be simply a variant of it. Pilate had sought to set up votive shields in his Jerusalem residence. The shields carried no images, but were inscribed, not unnaturally, with the name of the emperor. Again an uproar resulted. A letter of protest to Tiberius from the Jewish authorities led the emperor to withdraw the shields to Cæsarea.[4]

The only other incident known to us occurred several years after the execution of Jesus, but it may be mentioned as illustrating the far from easy task which Pilate had constantly found it to maintain order and better the province it had fallen to him to govern. A complaint was made to Vitellius, the governor of the province of Syria, that Pilate's soldiers had attacked a group of Samaritans near Gerizim, had slain many, and imprisoned and executed others. The claim was that these men had assembled peaceably to follow a man up the mountain to unearth the sacred utensils of the temple which had lain concealed since the days of Moses. Although the crowd had been heavily armed, which fact may well have made Pilate skeptical as to the innocence of their real purpose, Vitellius, without attempting himself to pass judgment, had at once relieved his junior colleague and sent him to Rome to make his defense to Tiberius. During the trip to Rome, Tiberius died. Pilate was not returned to his province and drops from history.[5]

It is against this background that the story reported in the gospels is to be considered. That the matter of this fanatic prophet, Jesus, who had left his native Galilee, had strayed

[3] Josephus, *Wars* 2, 9, 4; *Antt.* 18, 3, 2.
[4] Philo, *Embassy to Gaius* 38 (§§ 299 ff.) 589–590M.
[5] Josephus, *Antt.* 18, 4, 1–2.

south into the Roman province, and had been arrested as a rabble-rouser and preacher of sedition and violence, was of any especial moment in the eyes of Pilate is unlikely. It was but one more of many such incidents that had made so difficult his task of preserving order, which was imperative, but without violence, which would be suicidal. Another of similar nature, involving another Jew, Barabbas,[6] had just taken place. Hearkening to the request of the native authorities for aid in ridding the scene of the fanatic who they were convinced was advocating the overthrow of law and order was a matter of little concern to the Roman. Here at least he would not find himself confronted by an enraged populace. Very possibly they were right in their estimate, but at any rate the removal of a mad fanatic, even if his menace had been exaggerated, was a matter of little consequence.

Thus to see Pilate racked by pangs of conscience, knowing that he was being forced to do a colossal wrong, is to look at the act in the light of what subsequent years proved its tremendous importance, and not through the eyes of a contemptuous Roman official who saw it as but one more chore which was his fate as the governor of those utterly incomprehensible Jews. There have been few more acute and incisive studies of the luckless Pilate than Anatole France's sketch, "The Procurator of Judea": What has seemed to most readers of the gospel story the one all-eclipsing incident in Pilate's whole career—and which in later legend was to haunt his remaining years of agonized wandering, until, in an effort to drown out the incessant word, "Thou hast crucified the Christ," he plunged headlong into the Swiss lake—may well have been of such little moment to

---

[6] The practice recorded in the gospels of the governor freeing one political prisoner each year "at the feast" (Mark 15:6; Matt. 27:15; John 18:39 ff.) is otherwise unknown.

Pilate himself that a few years later he had quite forgotten
the event or even the name of the Jew whom he had so un-
concernedly condemned.

It is by no means certain that the precise charge to Pilate
was: "This man claims to be the king of the Jews, and thus
is a rival to the emperor," as our accounts might seem to suggest. Rather the charge would seem to have been: "a sedi-
tious and dangerous madman, inciting the lower classes to
revolution and violence." Of course if, as seems likely, Jesus'
term for the new age soon to dawn had been "the kingdom
of God," the seemingly simple deduction may have been
reached that a kingdom implied a king. But if so, we cannot
tell whether that was the conclusion of the governor himself, to whom Jewish apocalypticism and its dreams may well
have been incomprehensible, or the suggestion of the Jewish
authorities themselves, who may honestly, if incorrectly, have
concluded that Jesus' pose as a prophet and his prediction
of the speedy advent of a greater "Son of man" were but
subterfuges to hide more dangerous ambitions.

All of this is at best uncertain. The point of importance,
however, is that none of the principals—Roman governor or
Jewish authorities—had made a detailed or dispassionate
"study of the case." It seemed to them all a dangerous plot
—one of but many—and to be promptly suppressed.

From the point of view of the Jewish authorities the danger was imminent. Were this fanatic insurrectionist to be
disregarded, at any moment his mob of followers might
break loose; in the ensuing bedlam Rome would most certainly intervene, and their own quasi freedom would be
over. After all, this was a matter which very definitely did
concern Rome. Failure to bring the potential menace to the
governor's attention while it could be checked might well
prove costly to them in the long run and lead to reprisals

and to stricter oversight. Moreover it would be a very smart move. Should there be an outbreak of protest from the self-styled prophet's supporters, far better that the object of the popular hatred be the Roman governor rather than they. Thus, regardless of whether legally they could or could not themselves inflict the death penalty, it was but common sense to let Pilate take the step.

From the point of view of Pilate the matter was equally clear. Should he refuse to follow the advice of the local leaders, who knew their tricky and incomprehensible fellow countrymen as no Roman ever could hope to do, and should this individual prove a serious menace, well might he tremble at the thought of his own fate at the hands of an outraged Tiberius. So with little concern or hesitation [7] Pilate "delivered Jesus, when he had scourged him, to be crucified." [8]

The sentence was speedily put into effect. Our accounts, despite the several touches, some of seemingly sober fact, others certainly evidencing the rapid growth of evaluation in what has been aptly styled "a kind of crucifixion drama," attempt no detailed description of a death by a torture which Cicero had styled a century before "the cruelest and most shocking form of execution." [9] To most readers their absence is little loss. Whether the surprisingly speedy death, which all the accounts imply, was due to bodily weakness, conceivably hastened by the scourging and subsequent manhandling by the warders,[10] or was expedited by other means

---

[7] The least convincing of the details in the story is the ludicrous terror of Pilate at the thought of incurring Jewish displeasure.

[8] Mark 15:15.

[9] . . . "crudellissimi tæterrimique supplicii"—*In Verrem* II, v, 64.

[10] To many this has seemed to explain why Jesus had not himself carried the crossbeam, as was commonly required of the condemned (cf. Plutarch, *De Sera Numinis Vindicta* 9 [2, 554A]). Others regard the detail of Simon of Cyrene, who was compelled to bear it for Jesus (Mark 15:21; Matt. 27:32; Luke 23:26), as a later legendary touch illustrating the injunction:

must remain, with so many other of the details of his life, at best uncertain. To some who ponder the scene, although from afar, the most terrible detail of all stands out in stark clearness—the cry of agony, not the result of the nails, if such chanced to have been used,[11] but of the collapse of the confidence which had been his throughout his ministry. God had failed him, or he had failed God! What had seemed so certainly the voice of God—at once a command and promise —had not been realized. The kingdom had not dawned. For him the sun was assuredly darkened and all earth's foundations shook. All that remained was a despairing "Why!" That an increasing host of followers in subsequent generations, were to strive faithfully, if at times feebly, to fulfill what they believed, rightly or wrongly, to be his one great purpose— to bring in and establish the kingdom, which he had believed would be brought in by God quite without their aid, or his —this he could not know. In a night in which all of the lamps had flickered out, Jesus "gave up the ghost."

"If any man would come after me, let him deny himself, and take up his cross, and follow me" (Mark 8:34). There is no mention of this act of Simon in the Fourth Gospel. Its omission may well be due to the Gnostic contention that it was Simon, not Jesus, who was actually crucified, the two having exchanged roles (Irenæus, *Adv. Hær.* 1, 24, 4).

[11] There is no mention of nails in the Synoptic account. John specifies them (20:20, 25, and 27), along with the gash in his side, as the proof of identity which Thomas required. Actually the detail of the "riven side," from which blood and water had flowed (John 19:34), is to be seen as the fulfillment of prophecy (Zech. 12:10), with the blood and water symbolically typifying the two sacraments, the eucharist and baptism, not a physiological symptom piquing medical diagnosis.

Epilegomena: *"We have seen the Lord"*

For NEARLY two thousand years these triumphant words of the other disciples to Thomas have been regarded, and rightly, as constituting the very core of the Christian gospel—at once the proof of the justice of its claims and the earnestness of its triumph. In contrast to the sadness and gloom of that awful Friday, with a cross silhouetted against the leaden sky, stands the joy of the Easter morning, with the stone rolled away from the chamber of death, and the words of heaven's messenger, who speaks not alone to the women who had come to weep over the broken body, but to us: "He is not here; he is risen."

The usual—to many the natural—understanding of the Easter hope, as it finds expression in these early stories, is in terms of a changed Jesus. To me there appears a far profounder change, without which our hopes would be dead: Not a changed Jesus, but changed disciples. Jesus was the same. He had sown his seed, had lived his life, had built

209

himself into the lives of those with whom he had lived and worked. Pilate's contemptuous reply to the Jewish leaders at the cross [1] is even truer of Jesus: What he had written, he had written. The change was not in any physical transformation of the body he had tenanted, but in the outlook and convictions of the men and women whom he had touched.

Between the last chapter of the Passion and the triumphant start of the early disciples in their newborn determination that when the Son of man returned he should find faith in the earth lies another chapter, only hinted at in our gospels and too often overlooked in our thinking. Only it can explain the otherwise insoluble enigma. And this chapter took place on the shores and hillsides of Galilee, not among the rock-hewn tombs of the nation's capital.

At the time of his arrest the disciples had fled in panic back to Galilee. Beneath the stories in the gospels this fact is still to be discerned. The bottom had dropped from life. Their house of cards had collapsed. Their dreams and hopes were over. But a few months before, as they had been about their daily tasks, this strange man had appeared. They had found themselves irresistibly drawn to him, had left their trades and homes to follow him. His dream had become theirs. They had come to share his conviction that God had finally made known his will; that even now the world was trembling; that soon, very soon, God himself would intervene, would establish an entirely new kind of life upon a new earth. This, the real fulfillment of Israel's many wistful dreams for the future, was speedily to come. The seed had been sown. The harvest must come.

When he had left Galilee for the nation's capital, they had followed. What the end might be they did not know. One thing they did know: cords which could not be broken

[1] John 19:22.

bound them to this man. Where he went, they must go too. Then had come those awful days. God's prophet of the new day had fallen. His enemies had triumphed. Their confidence had been but an empty dream. In the bleakness of that dreadful moment they fled to their homes: "We had hoped that it was he who should redeem Israel." What was to be the outcome? Would that first numbing grief triumph? With its passing would the still more damning verdict be reached: A beautiful dream while it lasted, but now vanished beyond recall?

Then something happened. In the place of bleak dispair there was a new and victorious confidence. But was it really *new?* So we have often explained the story: "Only a miracle could have rolled that stone away. Had not Jesus in physical form stood before them again, had they not seen him with physical eyes, touched him with hands of flesh, they could never have regained their confidence."

Does not such an easy and seemingly natural view fail completely to appreciate the power of such a life as his? They "saw the Lord." Indeed yes; but was it the one with nail-pierced hands, or was it the one with whom they had lived and labored? Did they not see him as he had stood by the side of the grief-stricken mother and had brought comfort? as he had faced the haughty leaders, and undaunted had challenged them to their faces? as he had gathered the children about him? as he had struggled alone with God on the mountainside in prayer? as he had talked with humbled publicans, with men and women at whom the proper people had pointed the finger of scorn? as he had stood before Pilate? as he had shared their evening meals? Back in these familiar scenes, everything spoke of him. As they sat at table, he was with them "in the breaking of bread."

Were they the same men who had toiled and fished? Had there not been a gradual change in them during the months? Had not Jesus built himself, unbeknownst to them and perhaps to him, into them so completely that he was even then living in them? To think that after such a fellowship they could remain untouched, unchanged, appears to me absurd. It would have been a greater miracle had they not seen him, for he was even then living in them. The body, which when taken down from the cross had been placed in a rock-hewn tomb, was not Jesus of Nazareth. The real Jesus was not the flesh and the blood and the bone and the skin, but that something which had the power to reproduce itself in them, that lived in them. How hard it is to learn that profoundest of all truths: the whole is far more than the sum of its parts! What makes me me, what makes you you, what made Jesus Jesus was that quality, that something, which no camera can photograph, no scales can weigh; that is one's to give but not to keep; that we are constantly giving to others, whether we will or not, and without it ever being thereby diminished.

If it is true of us—and I believe profoundly that it is—that our lives are like the proverbial pebble thrown into the sea, which causes ripples to go wider and wider until they reach the farthest shore, even though the most delicate instruments may soon fail to detect their presence; if it is true that nothing in the universe is ever lost, that every word we speak, every act we perform, has the potential to continue endlessly, for good or for ill, in the lives of others: who, then, will wish to prescribe limits for the reproductive power of a compelling personality such as that of Jesus upon those privileged for months to have been with him? Who will find it incredible that during those days in Galilee, where everything was alive and vibrant with him, where uppermost in their minds were the memories of what he had said, what he had done, that gradually the first grief and shock gave way and in their place there arose the inevitable confidence that he had not been—could not have been—thwarted, that instead they had failed tragically to comprehend? God had sent him for a task. God could not be stayed. He was now with God but would soon return. Their task was to carry on.

In his constant reference to the one who would come at any moment to consummate the history of the world, to usher in the new age, he had not, as they had blindly thought, meant another. He had, instead, meant himself. God's prophet was none other than God's final judge. He would speedily return, would usher in the age which with divine insight he had so constantly and insistently proclaimed. In the interim they must not fail. His mantle, his spirit, was now theirs.

With this confidence, a confidence not built upon ecstatic visions—though it may well have led to them—but upon the solid and unshakable foundation which had been wrought in them through their companionship with him, they eventually returned to Jerusalem to a task they now saw was still unfinished. Through the years Christians have commemorated what they style the "Triumphal Entry": people crying, "Blessed be he that cometh in the name of the Lord," as Jesus rides into the city. They throw down palm branches and with them their garments, but a few days later their voices are stilled. In their place echoes a terrible shriek: "Crucify, crucify."

Is *that* the triumphal entry? Christianity has a triumphal entry, but it was not that pitiful scene, so pathetically phrased:

> "Ride on! ride on in majesty!
> In lowly pomp ride on to die."

Instead, it is the scene that no one has ever sought to describe, when the little group of men who had found themselves, with none to hail their advent, re-entered with radiant confidence the city which had crucified their Master, and which might well do the same to them.

Surely none will be so blind as to see in their return the desire to verify their new-found confidence, to prowl around the rock-cut tombs for evidence that that body was not there. They had no thought nor need to seek the living among the dead. They knew he lived, that he was now with God. As prophets of God, they too, as had he, commenced the task of heralding the approaching day. But now there was a new note in their preaching. This Jesus, whom wicked men had crucified in their vain attempt to stay God's purposes and plans, had not lain a prey to death, but had risen, was even now at God's right hand, and would speedily return to establish the kingdom which he had so passionately proclaimed.

They too, as had their leader before them, encountered opposition. Their claim that he had risen was by many contemptuously dismissed. But by others it found acceptance and was repeated and paraphrased again and again by the ever-increasing number of early preachers. Gradually as the years went by this message became embodied in stories which sought to give pictorial form to this firmly held confidence. An empty tomb, a stone rolled away, angelic figures —all these gradually took shape.

The eternal Easter hope, however, is not contained in these later stories, which sought, as an answer to not unnatural and incredulous disbelief, to explain *how* he had been raised or *how* he had ascended into heaven; but rather in the fact that we have one whom we call Lord, who during the days of his flesh lived in such a manner that those who had known him best *knew* that he had not been thwarted, and who found it easier to deny the stubborn facts of experience than to doubt his triumph. This early seal of approval, this discerning appraisal of the real power and purpose of God in terms of such a life, not the opportunity afforded a Thomas to put his fingers into the prints of the nails, his hand into the wounded side, is what leads us to echo his cry: "My Lord and my God."

Every attempt to remove him from us, to make of him an alien visitor—in the world but not of the world—attended at his every step by angelic hosts ready to perform for him tasks they would not perform for the rest of mankind, tends to deny that profoundest of insights, that "in all things he was made like unto his brethren." None of us, despite our easy recital of the Apostles' Creed, expects at our death to be raised after three days supernaturally from the grave. That such a vindication of his work was necessary to compel men to see the significance of his life, appears to me to strike an alien note and to paralyze us in our attempt to perform the tasks in our day which he has called us to do. But if we can believe that that drive to life, that universal and unsatisfied longing which pervades and dominates the universe to its core, and which through the ages men have called God, reveals itself in all its power and potential purpose in men who grasp it unafraid and seek to wrest its secrets, learn its laws, obey its rules; that within us there is a power of discernment which enables us to distinguish things which differ and to prefer things which excel, as we do the tasks to which we too are called—then in sober fact our house is built upon a rock which can never be shaken. The one whom we call Lord, who stands for us the compelling expression of the longings and dreams of mankind, by the quality of his life, by his unflinching bravery and devotion, by his fidelity to his task, transformed his followers, not by miracles which he wrought nor by miracles which were later wrought upon him, but by the life which he lived—transformed them into men like himself, who recognized him for what he was, and thus saw God in him.

On every hand we find ourselves confronted with doubts. Is life worth the living? What is the point of trying to live in the uplands? What evidence is there that a life spent in any sort of service has the slightest effect on the unthinking, heedless, so unresponsive folk with whom we rub shoulders? Were it not better to withdraw, like Horace's miser, and count our coins in secret? Against these doubts, by which all of us are at times assailed, there stands the figure of the Prophet from Nazareth, who by his life has left us both the proof that men, however heedless, however blind they may be, do have sufficient of the divine insight to see in such a life the very impress of God himself, and the challenge to do in our day an equivalent of what he did in his.

Have the years taken him from us? Are we to feel that since he walked the hillsides of Galilee amid circumstances far different from our own, was of different race from us, was concerned with problems, many of which for us do not exist, dreamed dreams that will not come to us, that he has no message for us? For many people today the answer is yes. They stand dismayed at the gulf which separates him from them. The comfortable old beliefs by which they had sought to bridge that ever-widening gulf have been taken away. Like Mary Magdalene, they come in sorrow to shed a final tear over him in farewell, and they cannot even find the body to weep over. The years have taken him away. Those who come to weep know not where they have laid him.

But when Mary wiped the tears from her eyes and turned around, there stood the ever-living Christ behind her, with hand raised in blessing. In this unforgettable picture the author of the Gospel of John has left us one of the world's great heritages—if we have eyes to see it aright. Jesus is not dead, but is living. Not the body which walked the Palestinian hills, but that essence of the divine that made Jesus Jesus; that quality which drew men to him, which transformed them, which enabled them to see aright the kind of life God wished them to live—that still lives. Jesus is not dead, can never die. He was never placed in any tomb, but has lived in the hearts and lives of the millions of men and women to whom he is endlessly calling, demanding that they follow with him to the only goal.

Appendix: *Useful Books*

No attempt is here being made to supply a bibliography which will be in any sense or degree complete. The scholar will not need such; the serious student will wish—or should be so encouraged—to make his own; the general nonprofessional reader would probably find it simply confusing. Instead, a few books are listed which for one reason or another I feel particularly useful for the general reader who may desire to extend his reading on this point or that. I have attempted to limit the books mentioned to those of more than ephemeral value and which are likely to be found in public libraries or easily to be obtained by interlibrary loan. I have further attempted to limit the list (with a very few exceptions) to volumes in English, thus listing translations, whenever they are available, even though a more complete edition in the original language subsequently appeared. Under the few main headings the books are listed alphabetically by authors, with no attempt thereby to indicate chronological sequence or comparative value. For the most part so-called "older Lives of Jesus"—those appearing during the nineteenth century—are not included. The significant ones are appraised in Schweitzer's invaluable *Quest of the Historical Jesus*. Many of them, not forgetting Strauss' revolutionary *Life of Jesus*, may still be studied with distinct profit by students mature enough to realize that "correctness of final conclusions" is far from being the sole—or even a very illuminating—criterion of values.

I. HISTORY AND SOURCES

R. H. Charles, *Apocrypha and Pseudepigrapha of the
    Old Testament.*
M. S. Enslin, *Christian Beginnings.*
C. Guignebert, *The Jewish World in the Time of Jesus.*

F. J. F. Jackson and K. Lake, *The Beginnings of Christianity*, VOL. I.

G. F. Moore, *Judaism*.

S. Perowne, *The Life and Times of Herod the Great*.

R. H. Pfeiffer, *History of New Testament Times, with an Introduction to the Apocrypha*.

E. Schürer, *A History of the Jewish People in the Time of Jesus Christ*.

II. GOSPELS

R. H. Lightfoot, *History and Interpretation in the Gospels*.

D. W. Riddle, *The Gospels*.

J. H. Ropes, *The Synoptic Gospels*.

B. H. Streeter, *The Four Gospels*.

R. V. G. Tasker, *The Nature and Purpose of the Gospels*.

III. INTRODUCTIONS TO THE NEW TESTAMENT

M. Dibelius, *A Fresh Approach to the New Testament and Early Christian Literature*.

M. S. Enslin, *Literature of the Christian Movement* (Part III of *Christian Beginnings* and available as a separate Harper Torchbook volume).

E. J. Goodspeed, *An Introduction to the New Testament*.

R. Heard, *An Introduction to the New Testament*.

A. Jülicher, *Introduction to the New Testament*.

A. H. McNeile, *An Introduction to the Study of the New Testament*.

J. Moffatt, *Introduction to the Literature of the New Testament*.

S. Sandmel, *A Jewish Understanding of the New Testament*.

IV. JESUS IN RESEARCH AND DEBATE

S. J. Case, *Jesus through the Centuries*.

J. G. H. Hoffmann, *Les Vies de Jesus et le Jesus de l'Histoire*.

C. C. McCown, *The Search for the Real Jesus*.

A. Schweitzer, *The Quest of the Historical Jesus*.

W. L. Sperry, *Jesus Then and Now*.

V. JESUS

G. Bornkamm, *Jesus von Nazareth*.

Appendix: Useful books

W. Bousset, *Jesus.*

H. J. Cadbury, *Jesus: What Manner of Man.*
The Peril of Modernizing Jesus.

M. Dibelius, *Jesus.*

M. Goguel, *The Life of Jesus.*

C. Guignebert, *Jesus.*

S. E. Johnson, *Jesus in his Homeland.*

J. Klausner, *Jesus of Nazareth.*

V. Taylor, *The Life and Ministry of Jesus.*

J. Warschauer (Warsaw), *The Historical Life of Christ.*

VI. SPECIAL SUBJECTS

W. E. Bundy, *The Psychic Health of Jesus.*

S. J. Case, *The Historicity of Jesus.*

M. Dibelius, *The Sermon on the Mount.*

J. Jeremias, *The Parables of Jesus.*

A. Jülicher, *Die Gleichnisreden Jesu.*

C. H. Kraeling, *John the Baptist.*

S. V. McCasland, *By the Finger of God.*

L. J. McGinley, *Form-Criticism of the Synoptic Healing
Narratives.*

A. Richardson, *The Miracle-Stories of the Gospels.*

A. Schweitzer, *The Mystery of the Kingdom of God.*

B. T. D. Smith, *The Parables of the Synoptic Gospels.*

J. Weiss, *Die Predigt Jesu vom Reiche Gottes.*

A. N. Wilder, *Eschatology and Ethics in the Teaching of Jesus.*

H. Windisch, *The Meaning of the Sermon on the Mount.*

S. Zeitlin, *Who Crucified Jesus?*